"I think it's the best encapsulation of humour in coaching that I have seen (and one of the best overviews of the science of humour).

Coaching is a creative process and as such is enhanced by playfulness. The more we understand about effective coaching, the clearer it becomes that coaching is improv for learning. This book provides an invaluable resource for professionals to bring laughter into the core of their practice".

**David Clutterbuck**, *Special Ambassador European Mentoring & Coaching Council; visiting professor Henley Business School*

"I have been in psychotherapy several times in my life and I cannot think of a single occasion when my therapist told a joke or used humour with me. On the other hand I did on many occasions try to make my therapist laugh. I guess there were many reasons for this, both conscious and unconscious, but when I did – I was occasionally successful – I felt a sense of connection. Of course I may have been trying to manipulate them away from painful material, as Camba Ludlow suggests, and no doubt that was sometimes the case as, but the feeling of joining in on the joke was one that felt human and satisfying.

These experiences, along with a slight feeling of guilt when laughing with of my own clients, made me very curious to read this book. It doesn't disappoint in its in-depth exploration of the history, meaning and structure of humour, as well as its use in psychoanalysis and coaching. Camba Ludlow shows us that humour can be used in many different ways, and can illicit many different responses.

Amongst other effects, it can subvert rigidity in thinking and burst the balloon of narcissism and pomposity, so has a useful role to play in coaching and psychoanalysis (including other forms of psychotherapy), as it brings us up short and helps us to face uncomfortable truths as well as encouraging us to experience the way we are all part of the flawed and vulnerable human race".

**Judy Ryde**, *PhD, psychotherapist and supervisor*

# Humour in Psychoanalysis and Coaching Supervision

Drawing from psychoanalytic principles, Ingela Camba Ludlow uniquely explores and endorses humour as a serious and essential practical tool in coaching, coaching supervision and psychotherapy, showing how, when successfully integrated, it can help clients navigate the most difficult professional and personal challenges.

Often misunderstood and not accepted in the academic arena, chapters in Part 1 begin by looking at the history and evolution of humour from the Ancient Greeks to the modern age, distinguishing different types of humour from each other, such as wit, sarcasm and pantomime. Freud believed humour to be the highest mechanism of the human psyche and the book continues to examine his relationship and use of humour in psychotherapy, looking at his personal correspondence and patient testimonials as well as how his contemporaries, such as Bion, applied humour in their practice. Moving from theory to practice, chapters in Part 2 show practitioners through case studies, exercises and examples how they can use humour in sessions with clients. Specifically addressing how to use humour ethically, how to remain neutral as the coach and how to use humour to address anxiety, express anger and offer alternative rationalisations, this book provides coaches with the practical tools to expand their coaching practice.

This interdisciplinary book will be essential reading for coaches, psychotherapists and counsellors looking to broaden their coaching supervision skill set, as well as those who are interested in how humour can promote personal and professional development through a psychoanalytic lens.

**Ingela Camba Ludlow** is a PCC ICF Coach, an EMCC credentialed coach, coach supervisor and psychoanalyst. She has 20 years of business experience and 15 years working in human development, training and coaching. Based in Mexico, she has partnered with clients in various countries in Latin America, the United States, Canada and Singapore.

# Humour in Psychoanalysis and Coaching Supervision

## From Life to Interventions

Ingela Camba Ludlow

Routledge
Taylor & Francis Group

NEW YORK AND LONDON

Image credit: © Getty Images

First published 2023
by Routledge
605 Third Avenue, New York, NY 10158

and by Routledge
4 Park Square, Milton Park, Abingdon, Oxon, OX14 4RN

*Routledge is an imprint of the Taylor & Francis Group, an informa business*

© 2023 Ingela Camba Ludlow

The right of Ingela Camba Ludlow to be identified as author of this work has been asserted in accordance with sections 77 and 78 of the Copyright, Designs and Patents Act 1988.

ISBN: 978-0-367-71492-5 (hbk)
ISBN: 978-0-367-72309-5 (pbk)
ISBN: 978-1-003-15431-0 (ebk)

DOI: 10.4324/9781003154310

Typeset in Optima
by codeMantra

**To Pepe and Beti**

Cami and Kari

# Contents

# Preface to humour: names, frames and games

Humour always needs a preface – "Have you heard the joke about....?" "Let me tell you a funny story?" "That reminds me when…".

And that reminds me of Gregory Bateson, one of the greatest thinkers of the 20th century, who I have been learning from for over 40 years. He did not often tell jokes, but one he did tell went like this:

> A computer enthusiast searched out the latest and most powerful computer in the world, and programmed it to answer the question, whether or not computers would be able to think like human beings. After a very long wait the computer printer started to hum and the enthusiast rushed over to watch what was the answer the computer was printing. here on the paper were the words:
> "Now that reminds me of a story…"

I think what the computer really said was "Now that reminds me of a story and it is very funny, do you want to hear it?"

Freud said dreams were the royal road to the unconscious and Bateson that stories were the royal road to understand relationships and patterns. Bateson helped us realise how we are trapped in dividing the world up into things and then become further trapped in the world of the names of things. We then stop noticing the "pattern that connects" and it is in the connections of patterns that the real beauty of nature and life resides.

We easily get caught in what Wittgenstein called "language games", and in the limiting frames of our constructed reality and the names of the names.

Bateson was also fond of quoting Lewis Carrol and Alice's adventures, including how the White Knight introduces his song:

> The name of the song is called "HADDOCKS' EYES."'
> 'Oh, that's the name of the song, is it?' Alice said, trying to feel interested.
> 'No, you don't understand,' the Knight said, looking a little vexed.
> 'That's what the name is CALLED. The name really IS "THE AGED AGED MAN."'
> 'Then I ought to have said "That's what the SONG is called"?' Alice corrected herself.
> 'No, you oughtn't: that's quite another thing! The SONG is called "WAYS AND MEANS": but that's only what it's CALLED, you know!'
> 'Well, what IS the song, then?' said Alice, who was by this time completely bewildered.
> 'I was coming to that,' the Knight said. 'The song really IS "A-SITTING ON A GATE": and the tune's my own invention.

The name is not the thing named, and the thing named has been constructed by our naming of it and by how our mind has created a mental boundary around a part of what it has perceived and separated this out from its context. In nature text and context are inseparable, mutually interconnected and in-dwelling. Humour uses human madness to interrupt the human madness of building mental constructs that we then imprison ourselves within and imagine they are the only reality.

Here is a surreal joke from the very stand-up comic, Steven Wright:

> "Last night somebody broke into my apartment and replaced everything with exact duplicates... When I pointed it out to my roommate, he said, "Do I know you?"

Steven Wright is playing with our sense of continuity and change in a similar way that Lewis Carrol does, when Alice is asked by the Caterpillar who she was, and replies that she knew this morning, but since then so much has changed since then, she no longer knows. Most of us, when asked who we are, we usually answer with what people have called us, or perhaps mention a few roles we have occupied, chosen to impress the other. We know at another level that it is not who we are, but, within the game of social convention, we know we are not lying. To not abide by these social convention games would be deemed to be mad, but it is also mad when we play the social convention game and believe that this is the reality.

In my book "*The Wise Fool's Guide to Leadership*" (Hawkins 2005), I draw on the perennial stories of Nasrudin, the archetypal wise fool, who taught through his foolishness. Ingela quotes some of the stories in this book. I was intrigued by the many Nasrudin stories I had collected as I went around the world and listened to spiritual teachers and taxi drivers, and those who were possibly both. It struck me that if Nasrudin entered the 21st century he would probably become a psychotherapist, consultant or executive coach, so I took the liberty of recasting many of the stories in organisations of today. In the book I try and show how:

> Nasrudin invites us to embrace paradox and to realize that causality is not a linear process but emerges from underlying interconnected patterns. Within the Sufi tradition the stories should work at least at three levels:
>
> - the creative jump of humour
> - the psychological shift in one's mindset, and
> - the spiritual dimension of releasing us temporarily from our personal fixity of being.
>
> A good Nasrudin story always has an after-taste or a good kick-back. The story slips into the house by its engaging good humor, but once inside it can start to re-arrange the furniture and knock new windows through the walls. This can be very releasing if you recognize the prison in which you often live, but very disconcerting if you have grown attached and comfortable in your institutionalized home.

Humour can help us with the frames through which we are looking and thinking, and which we have previously taken for granted. It can use paradox and double meaning to loosen our fixed beliefs and mindsets. Nasrudin, and also King Lear's fool, could well be described by Viola's description in William Shakespeare's play "Twelfth Night" (Act III, Scene 1):

> "*This fellow is wise enough to play the fool;*
> *And to do that well craves a kind of wit:*

*He must observe their mood on whom he jests,*
*The quality of persons, and the time,*
*And like the haggard, check at every feather*
*That comes before his eye. This is a practice*
*As full of labour as a wise man's art:*
*For folly that he wisely shows is fit;*
*But wise men folly-fall'n, quite taint their wit".*

Humour also can help us loosen our fixed self-narratives, the old stories we tell ourselves and others about who we think we are. Gentle teasing can help us see the incongruity between what we say and what we do, and it can prick our pomposity, help us laugh at ourselves and gradually become less narcissistic. As Barry Oshry points out in his wonderful book seeing systems, when "stuff" happens at work we take it personally but 95% of what happens is not personal, we just fail to see the bigger picture. However, as Ingela points out it is essential that we start by laughing at ourselves, before we laugh at others and indeed the ability to self-comment humorously on one's own current behaviour I would see as an essential skill for all psychotherapists, coaches and supervisors. The best way to start every day is to look in the mirror and have a good laugh at whoever looks back at you.

Ingela helps us on the journey towards being "wise-enough to play the fool" and develops the practice that takes practice. She also shows how humour used by the psychotherapist, coach or supervisor can have many other beneficial aspects, as well as the ones, mentioned above, such as:

- Normalizing our experience and inviting us to see our common humanity
- Helping us approach difficult feelings and events in a softer, less direct way.
- A joint release of tension.
- To provide a safe enough play space to experiment with new perspectives and new ways of being.
- To see the same event from multiple perspectives.

The great Sufi teacher Hazrat Inayat Khan showed how a true Sufi or wise person, always sees any issue or event from more than one perspective, and indeed much of the distress that turns up in the therapy or coaching sessions, originates from the stories we have created about what has happened and our rigid attachment to them. To do good work, we have to loosen our attachment to our narratives, before we can begin to create new possibilities and new options for moving forward.

Ingela also points to the shadow side of using humour in our work. These include:

- How humour can be used as a defence against fully allowing oneself to feel and experience something, either by the client or the helping professional trying to resist fully letting in an experience that needs to be faced.
- How it can be used as a seductive manoeuvre by either party.
- Can come from a compulsive need to show off, perform or entertain the other.
- Can be used as a way of caricaturing the other in a way that labels them and/or puts them one-down. She shows how this can border on the sadistic.

Humour can also be a way of communicating something indirectly, while denying ownership and responsibility for what was said, by retorting when challenged – "I was only joking!"

We need to be watchful for these potential shadow aspects of humour, but not avoid the richness that humour can open for us. Without humour the world would be flat and we would find it harder to escape the prison of our fixed ways of thinking, doing and being.

I wrote in my notebook when still under 20 years old:

"We should take ourselves seriously and laugh at the world, rather we should take life seriously and laugh at ourselves for so doing". When you can do this all you need is a mirror either in therapy, coaching, super-vision or in your bathroom, to be able to have a lot of fun!

Thank you Ingela, for a book that shows the rich history of understanding the nature of humour and the many diverse ways psychoanalysts, psychotherapists, coaches and coach supervisors have taught how, and how not, to use humour, at the learning edge, where we discover what is knocking at our door.

Now that reminds me of a joke!

*Professor Peter Hawkins,*
*Barrow Castle Bath March 2021*

# Acknowledgements

This book is possible because of a strong beautiful network that guided me and/or contained me with humour and laugh at the times when the endeavour seemed too ambitious.

Thanks to my parents Jose Luis and Beatriz that from the awakening of life until now have taught me with their example of wit, humour and compassion. Humour without compassion would not have been a tool for the self. Thanks also to my sister Ursula for her wit and countless hours of laugh making sisterhood not only loving but fully enjoyable. Thanks to Camila and Karina, they shared part of the timing because as they were growing up they reminded me what playing is about, and what is the sound of a child laughing with pleasure.

I had been very lucky to have the best wisest teachers in my dearest professions coaching and psychoanalysis. To Norberto Bleichmar and Elena Ortiz that guided me throughout my first research on humour many years ago, their openness, kindness and deep knowledge in clinical psychoanalysis. In coaching, Peter Hawkins has been a true inspiration, sharing with his wisdom and humour his system of taking the world on the environment and preserving it for future generations. Damian Goldvarg taught me the beauty of Coaching Supervision.

Thanks to Judy Ryde and David Clutterbuck for their kind reading and generous words towards the text.

Thanks to Miriam Martinez my writing coach and Barbara Toledo for her translation, for the endless hours and the rush. Thanks to Alfonso Araujo for being my attentive my rigourous and elegant style corrector, and thanks especially for all the laughs.

And finally but very importantly, this work is possible because my patients and clients have taught me quite things about seriousness and laughs, of falling and recovering and being able to walk with a smile.

# Introduction

The search for humour has a personal history for me. Humour can appear in any area of human life and it can even save lives.

My father lost his father when he was three and a half years old, at a time when it was difficult for a woman to support a family. In spite of some difficult moments, such as when it was impossible to renew school uniforms every year, the strictness of the teachers, the difference in the pastimes and travels of family and friends, my father always had a humorous and happy tale to tell about this period. Even if the tragedy of becoming an orphan has always lingered, his life has not been a dramatic one, but rather a journey in which humour has always accompanied him. From him, I learned that it is fundamental to expand the use of humour in all walks of life. I think it is important to see it as a healthy topic as well as an exploration. Then what could be better than to put it to use in practices such as psychotherapy, coaching, supervision or other related professions?.

Freud (1980) ends his 1895 article *Studies on Hysteria* by telling a patient at the end of their first session of analysis: "you will be convinced that we are making good progress if we can manage to transform your hysterical distress into common misfortune" (p. 168). One must ask if Freud wasn't his own worst promoter scaring off his patients with such words of comfort. Of course, at the end of the 19th century the fantasy that well-being lay within the reach of anyone, did not exist. Today, if one decides to submit to analysis, like the above patient, what sort of a promise would that be? Freud's joke implies the idea that there is a gulf between hysterical distress and common misfortune. We have the clue as to how the humour in this case hides the possibility of something

DOI: 10.4324/9781003154310-1

better, and this possibility might tempt us to venture to find that "something better" through analysis.

I started this research intrigued by those who have made humour a way of relating to life. Many questions arise: How is it that some people have it (a sense of humour) or master it? Is it a position? If humour makes life so pleasant, then how can this be reflected in the process of an analysis? Is it part of it? What are its limitations?

It is evident that humour has been mostly restricted outside of social context or entertainment. It is not a discursive form in supposedly rigorous studies: academia is the best example of this. In most disciplines, we find rigorous guidelines which are followed solemnly. This solemnity, devoid of humour, seems to annihilate curiosity and in the intent of formulating a thought the very essence of what we were seeking or creating is lost. The same happens in psychoanalysis, which has created its halo of sobriety. Giovacchini (1999), a psychologist living in the United States, tells us how during the 60s the meetings of analysts were held in an almost funeral atmosphere, "bearded analysts, smoking fat cigars, making profound judgements with a solemnity that made it seem that the future of civilization was at risk" (p. 89). Of course, psychoanalysis is serious, but there is no need for it to be sombre. The same about the helping professions, we are in the field of taking care of others in a professional and dedicated way, we are serious about it, there is no need to devoid it from humour. It is also the case for living.

This book can be read in different ways. It is composed of three parts. As a personal preference, I thought it interesting to start with the cultural aspects related to the history and the essence of humour itself and its distinctiveness with other humorous forms (Part I). Not an easy task and it might feel like an arbitrary choice, but we have to start from somewhere!. Then it is followed by a revision of humour in psychotherapy and psychoanalysis, with the analysis on its form and mechanisms based on each of these lines of thought (Part II). Then it is followed by how it can be used in Coaching and Coaching Supervision with specific tools on reflecting on humour, examples on to introduce humour during the sessions and clear humour dont's (Part III). However, the reader can jump directly to Part II or Part III and decide to later visit the other segments of the text. It depends on how rapidly or how deeply the audience requires to learn about humour to introduce it in their practice or leadership style.

This book is intended for the helping professions: therapists, psychologists, coaches, supervisors, coaching supervisors, conflict facilitators, caretakers, etc. However, it is an invitation to the broader audience to invite humour in their lives, in their families, their classes, their meetings and their conversations where appropriate. And then the natural question is: What is appropriate? It is time to start reading this book.

# Man and the history of humour

Knowledge is temperance for the young, consolation for the old,
wealth for the poor and ornament for the rich.
Diogenes

What the word humour describes/means has undergone important variations over time. The first time we come across it is in the medical writings of Hippocrates where he establishes the existence of basic humours in the human body that constitute the causes of diseases (Pollock, 2003, p. 15). This meaning is still valid: in the Oxford Universal Dictionary, one of the first definitions of humour is: "any fluid or juice of an animal or plant…". This is not likely to be the one we had in mind, but it gives us a clue as to its origin being at the heart of the word humour. Further on, we find humour in reference to people and what they say, write, draw, etc. as a consistent quality describing or showing the comic or ridiculous side of things or persons with or without malice.

Humour as a bodily fluid or humour relative to a person's actions? How has this great leap in the meaning of the word humour come about? To begin to understand it, we have to start with Greek history and take as a guiding thread the various manifestations linked to laughter, comedy and humour in different periods in time.

In this quest, I shall pause, indistinctly, at various notions such as comedy, laughter, sarcasm, invective, etc. All these are different instances that variously relate to humour (differences will be dealt with in the following chapter), as well as the concepts of love and pain which as we will see, are also part of this history.

We could actually think of the history of humour as a guiding thread in the history of mankind.

DOI: 10.4324/9781003154310-2

# Antiquity

Hippocrates (460-370 B.C.) is considered to be the first physician. The basis of his theory states that a general humour-like fluid exists which flows through the whole body and has four qualities. These are bile, black bile, phlegm and blood, and the imbalance of these is the cause of illness.

In the particular case of black bile, the word *melancholy* describes both a fluid (black bile) and a state of mind, an emotional state (melancholy). Melancholia at that time was described as a state of sadness and fear, a meaning which remains to this day. Later on, melancholia would be the predecessor of depression, but there is still a long way to go before that.

At about this time, the encounter between medicine and laughter took place, at least in the Western world, represented by Hippocrates and the atomist Democritus of Abdera (ca. 460-370 B.C.). Democritus governed the city of Abdera for ten years, he was a well-respected man who in his old age retired to study and think calmly in his villa. Something about this isolation disturbed the senators to the point of considering him mad, so they summoned Hippocrates to visit him. During the encounter Democritus' exaggerated laughter seemed incomprehensible to Hippocrates, who scolded him – he may have been rather alarmed – ordering him to suppress this laughter, since to laugh at all things implied that one could not distinguish between good and bad.

Democritus' response was as follows:

> when you have understood, laughter will seem to you and your people a better remedy and medicine (...) and you will be able to pass this knowledge on to others. When you have realized how much effort and dedication men spend on insignificant things, endeavouring to do worthless acts, consuming their lives with ridiculous things (...) you will think there are two causes for my laughter, a good one and a bad one. But I'm only laughing at man, his senselessness, his inability to act with rectitude, his puerile, local behaviour towards others; his pointless submission to countless hardships, his journeying to the ends of the earth (...) searching tirelessly for gold

and silver, endeavouring to acquire ever more worldly goods, so as not to be among the last to free himself of the shame of not being considered a happy man.

(Joubert, 2002, p. 182)

The dialogue between these two continued, and at the end, Hippocrates was no longer the same man, as it always happens when there has been a good conversation. In his report to the senate, he declared:

Democritus is not mad, but rather he is the wisest of us all. He has made us wiser, and through us, all humanity.

(Joubert, 2002, p. 179)

Democritus was outside conventions and this was a contrast to his former life because he had been a statesman who organised others and lived himself by the law. So as not to weep over the misfortune of man's banalities this man laughed, but it was a bitter laughter, and thus he turned it into an expression of wisdom.

G. Minois (2000) asked if this great laughter of Democritus' was the most appropriate response. If nothing made any sense, wasn't mockery the only reasonable attitude? Laughter seemed to be the only way to make life bearable since no other explanation seemed convincing.

Around the 4th century B.C., the philosophical and cultural movement known as Cynicism appeared.

The Cynics did not teach nor was there an institutional head of the movement, so one cannot call it a school. Its philosophy was not based on academic lecture, but it rather consisted in the imitation of exemplary figures (Bracht, 2000, p. 13), amongst them, Antisthenes (ca. 444-365), a disciple of Socrates, and Diogenes (ca. 413-327), the best-known disciple of Antisthenes. Of their vision, only fragments remain: daring and paradoxical testimonials with a singular sense of humour which attempt to reveal the truth. Their proposal about the relation of man to the world implied subversion of the established order. The examples they practised and the questions they posed are stark and reveal the absurdity and arbitrariness of the social convention. They exposed the false division between the nature of animals and that of humans. This meant that society finds itself in conflict with nature and that values such as religion, politics and ethics are false and counterproductive. Thus, he strongly criticised his fellow citizens who allowed themselves to be tormented by unimportant things. It is nature that should condition the ethical norm, and this is observable in animals based on real, vital necessities (eating, sleeping, procreating and defecating). The word Cynic comes from the Greek *kinikos* which means dogs. They were called dogs because they were frank and direct (to bark), for their ability to distinguish between friend and foe and their manner of living in public, like dogs "unashamedly indifferent" to the most rooted social norms (Bracht, 2000, p. 15).

Unfortunately, there are no remains of the most important written works of Cynic literature – they did exist according to Diogenes Laërtius, so we have to be satisfied with fragments mentioned by intermediaries.

> At a dinner, there were some who threw bones to him as if to a dog, and he drawing closer to them urinated on them like dogs do.
>
> To some youths who were nearby they said "take care that he doesn't bite us", he replied "don't worry boys, a dog doesn't eat greens".
>
> (Laercio, 2006, p. 193)

The Greek Cynics confronted the seats of learning and power. Their freedom was active, they practised it. They constantly tried to invade tradition through parody and satire in provocative acts of free expression directed at the existing authorities, such as Plato[1] and Alexander the Great.[2]

Therefore, they denounced and ridiculed the habits of their fellow citizens: "Entering a not very clean bath house, he asked the bathers who were there, 'where do you wash yourselves?'"(Laercio, 2006, p. 193). The decadence of man when he submits to pleasure: "Having seen a sign at the entrance to the house of a rich man that said 'For Sale', he said 'I knew that you would soon vomit your owner because of his immoderate drunkenness'" (Laercio, 2006, p. 193).

According to J. Moles, an enthusist of the cynics says a cynic is somebody in search of a virtuous life. It can be found anywhere and that is why he feels inclined towards the natural world and animals, and this makes him consider himself a citizen of the world. He accepts his relationship with other wise men and his potential kinship with humanity in general, whom he is trying to convert. He is a mediator between men and the gods, and his mediation constitutes an important part of his teaching activity. Stoicism is enriched by cynicism (Bracht, 2000, p. 159).

In the early Middle Ages, the same ambivalent attitude was adopted towards the first Christian authors as towards the Cynics, wavering between condemnation and praise. Their strongest critic was Saint Augustine (354–430) who recriminated them for their lack of decency and modesty. We should remember that they went about with the minimum of clothing and had sexual relations in public, but he accepted their ascetic style of life. So, on the one hand, they were respected and admired by Saint Jerome or Saint Augustine and, on the other hand, they were roundly condemned by personalities such as Simoni Apolinar and C. Mamerto (Bracht, 2000, p. 328). What is important is that the Cynic was a familiar element in the Middle Ages, whose legacy is due to pagan and Christian Latin authors as well as Arab sources. *El Mukhtar al hi-kam wa-mahasin al-kalim* (1048–1049) quoted Diogenes (Bracht, 2000, p. 315). In contrast, Erasmus in its *Apopthegmata* (beginning of 15th C.) considered that the graceful, amiable tone of words used by the Cynics made them perfectly adequate for educating princes and young men because this would lead easily to more rigorous learning (p. 328).

However, it is not his method of invective or sarcasm that makes Diogenes a model for the Christian philosophers of the Middle Ages, but rather his austere way of life: his detachment from material goods and disdain of wealth and honours. He followed a strict vote of poverty.

The evangelists are very severe about laughter and mockery. There is no mention of Jesus Christ laughing, while mockery was a mean of mistreating him. During his passion, the soldiers mocked him saying: "Hail, king of the Jews". The Athenian philosophers also mocked Saint Paul when he went to speak to them. In this way, a dialectic is established, although not articulated, that to be on the side of mockery and laughter is to be with those who mocked and laughed at Christ and his teachings. Some of the patriarchs of the Church in the high Middle Ages launched a ferocious attack on laughter. Tertulian was against comedies that he considered demonic or lewd; Basil of Cesarea wrote that laughter was not allowed in any circumstance; Saint Augustine considered that laughter was inconvenient, that it was against the teachings of Christ and, above all, it was diabolical (Minois, 2000, p. 208).

The book *The Name of the Rose* portrays this ecclesiastical posture towards laughter in these early Middle Ages. In this novel, there is a book that sets off a series of actions that end in tragedy. It's about a hypothetical *Book of Laughter* written by Aristotle. Those interested in the forbidden book die off one by one. Old George, deacon of the monastery and guardian of the fear of God, justifies himself saying:

> Laughter is a weakness, a corruption, the insipidness of our flesh. It is the entertainment of the peasant, the licence of the drunkard [... but] here [in the lost text] the function of laughter is inverted, it is elevated to an art, it opens vistas to a world of the learned, it becomes an object of philosophy, and of theological perfidy [...]. This book could trigger the spark that would ignite a new fire that would spread to the whole world; laughter would become a new art, even disregarding Prometheus, and capable of annihilating fear.
>
> (Eco, 2000, p. 467)

This is to say, laughter *per se* had no value, it belonged to the uneducated and ignorant, as if it were bad manners, but a work created by the respected Greek philosopher changed everything and set laughter on a level with art.

It is thus that the expressions of irony and humour as a method for teaching and denouncing disappear from the realm of religion and we need to seek them in the literature of what is known as low society, where it hid away from the eyes of the Church.

## The high Middle Ages

During the Middle Ages, scholarly thinking was dominated by religion, but everyday life had a series of characters that carried out secular cultural work, though unfortunately not much has survived. They belonged to different regions and with minor differences, these are the *Goliards*, *troubadors* and minstrels, who, under different forms of writing such as the *fabliaux*, *fratrasies*, romances, etc. portrayed and satirised different elements of everyday medieval life.

First, we find the Goliards, who were members of the lay clergy and were allowed to live far from their monasteries. They were students who could read and write and travelled from one place to another. They visited taverns, they liked feasting and they earned their livelihood by reciting poetry and singing drinking songs. Their texts had a philosophical bent and their work was the part of the Church that lived among the population in general. *They spread all over Europe without law or faith … but without humours* (Rouvière, 2005, p. 17). Carmina Burana is a collection of Goliard works, although it only deals with a selection of texts on love. These persons were the precursors of the troubadours and the *trouveres*. It is important to mention that both Goliards, as well as troubadours and trouveres, were minstrels who relied on mockery. They observed life in general and the people around them and from this observation, they developed their satirical texts and songs.

The troubadours were poets and singers who spoke Occitaine (*Langue d'Oc*). They belonged to the nobility and therefore had a high level of education. They were well versed in *the trivium* (grammar, rhetoric and logic) and the *quadrivium* (arithmetic, geometry, music and astronomy), this made them counsellors to kings. Among the first troubadours, we find William IX, Duke of Aquitaine (1071–1127) who, as well as attending to matters of state, was known for his female conquests and for being a great narrator of amusing anecdotes and jokes (Rouvière, 2005, p. 19).

There were also the *trouveres* (Rouvière, 2005, p. 21), who cultivated the genre called *fatrasies,* which were proverbs or verses flowing with contrived, elaborate language. It is said that they stimulated the humours, which is why they are included in the development of humour. There is more to this than a mere play on words. In the following chapters, we will see how humour is also a matter of context and also how word games are intrinsic to the human development of humour. A nonsense play on words being a modest glimpse of humour can lead to laughter or at least a smile. The following is a fragment of one of the playful verses of Jehan Bodel d'Arras (13th C.):

*Un ours emplumé*
*Fit semer du blé*
*De Douvres à Ouessant.*
*Un ognion pelé*
*S'etait appreté*
*A chanter devant*

*Quand sur en èlèphant rouge*
*Vint un limacon armé*
*Qui leur criait:*
*Fils de putains, arrivez!*
*Je versifie en dormant.*

*A feathered bear*
*Sowed wheat*
*From Dover to Ouessant.*
*A peeled onion*
*Was pressed*
*To sing in front*
*When on in a red hat*
*Came an armed slug*
*Who shouted at them:*
*Son of whores,*
*come on!*
*I versify while sleeping.*
    *(Rouvière, 2005, p. 23)*

In this same period, we find minstrels like Rutebeuf (1230–1290) a public entertainer who lived off his plays, in which he criticised contemporary figures such as prelates, ministers, physicians and men of law. In his plays, he didn't spare the ignorant masses who can be led to believe anything because they understand nothing (Minois, 2000, p. 182). However, he did not limit himself to criticism but also reflected on himself and the difficulties of his wandering life (Rouvière, 2005, p. 25).

*Je crois que Dieu le débonnaire*
*M'aime de loin!*

*I believe the Good Lord*
*Loves me from a distance*

During the 13th century, a new genre appeared, particularly in France: the *fabliaux*. These were octosyllabic verses whose content was often brutal, cynical, vulgar and even obscene. They were mostly anonymous and written in a mocking tone designed to cause laughter. Contrary to what one would think these verses were not intended for the masses but for the gentry: nobles and burghers for whom they were read in court circles and sometimes even in public squares (Minois, 2000, p. 172). The butt of their attacks did not vary much from other forms mentioned: priests, peasants, cuckolded husbands, misers and also the sick. The shortest *fabliaux* have a few dozen verses and the longest can reach up to a 1,000 verses. The text of the *Roman de Renart*, whose characters are mostly animals, belongs to this genre. It is a parody involving violence and sex, where instincts are not controlled by Christian morality and the text itself was in fact composed by various authors (Minois, 2000, p. 181).

In 1337, the Hundred Years' War between France and England made the nobles stop playing courtly games as they went to war. Since they were the ones who usually sponsored poets and artists, this period saw a decline in literary creation, including humour and comedy. Eustace Deschamps – also known as Maurel (1346-?) – is a notable exception. This author, as was the custom of the period, was ruthless in his descriptions. But according to J. Rouvière, he went even further because he used black humour for the first time (five centuries before J. Karl Huysmans invented the expression). We refer to a scene where a serf addresses his feudal Lord in the *Dialogue among beggars*.

> *Sire, I cannot lay me down (he has no bed)*
> *The lord replies:*
> *You have my permission to remain standing*
> *Further on: Sire, I do nothing but languish, give me something*
> *Just think, if you die, everything that you might have will be lost.*
> (Rouvière, 2005, p. 33)

In the above passage, commiseration is replaced by cynicism (note the use of the word). Black humour appears in the 14th century with E. Deschamps, in a century blackened by war and the plague.

In the Middle Ages, there is a resurgence in public entertainment where actors and audience mix. These street shows were the origins of farce in theatre, which will reappear intermittently in literature from Molière to Ionesco.

Farce draws topics previously used in the *fabliaux* and it engages in realistic portrayals of the society of that era. However, it was until some time later that satire of these scenes from everyday life was added.

When satire was directed to politics was the first time that humour carried a message (Rouvière, 2005, p. 49).

It was the time between the Middle Ages and the Renaissance when the burlesque mode appeared with Rabelais in *Gargantua and Pantagruel*. This novel in four volumes was published between 1532 and 1552. François Rabelais was the first to conceive of a work based on a type of humour that becomes degraded. When faced with the impossibility of reaching the truth, laughter is used to overcome interior fears as it cheerfully confronts transcendental problems such as life and death (Fajardo, 2002, p. 8). Rabelais himself writes a dedication to his readers:

*Friends who are starting to read me,*
*Do not do so out of mere affectation,*
*Nor as you read be scandalised;*
*The book contains no infection,*
*Although neither is it perfection.*
*If you do not learn, it will make you laugh,*
*I cannot choose another argument*
*In face of your insane pain.*
*To cause laughter not tears I want to write,*
*Since to laugh is the more human [...]*
    *(Rabeleais, 2005, p. 19)*

Milan Kundera calls this novel the *exceptional birth of a new art form*. In Rabelais' book, one can find everything: *the believable and the unbelievable, allegories and satire, giants and normal people, anecdotes and meditations, real and fantastic voyages, erudite dalliances, digressions of verbal virtuosity ... the communion of serious with terrible matters* (1994, p. 11). But not only this, he also considers that this text becomes clearly and radically a novel the moment it becomes *a territory where moral judgement is suspended* (pp. 14–15). This means a place where we are not dealing with exemplary heroes who do good or evil, but rather autonomous characters that make their own laws. The birth of the novel moves through humour.

# The Renaissance and wit

In French literature, the period from the beginning of the Renaissance up to the 17th century belongs to Molière, Racine and Corneille. As J. Rouvière says, Molière is not merely the prince of laughter, but the king. This stems from his magisterial effect on his audience, not only through his words but also through his scenic effects. There are comic gestures, which exist in pantomime, apparitions intended to ridicule characters and expose their defects. In Molière's plays, the scenic effects are often more important than the script. There are many clearly humourous moments as in *L'Amour Medecin* (1665):

… She died of four physicians and two apothecaries …

Or in Les Femmes Savantes (1671), Chrysele, the bourgeois husband of Philaminte (wise woman?), said:

To reason is the occupation of all my household,
And reasoning has displaced reason.

(Molière, 2005, p. 69)

In both cases, he is mocking what is supposedly culture or science when they border on the loss of common sense, showing that so much sophistication has deteriorated thought.

In 1579, Laurent Joubert, a French physician, published what is considered to be the most famous work about laughter. Joubert was very curious about laughter and questioned what it was, what its purpose was and what the effects on the human body were. He did not accept that it was something natural, but rather something extraordinary and surprising. So he made exhaustive studies on the effects laughter had on the heart, diaphragm, voice, face (eyes, nose and lips), arms, shoulders, feet, belly, etc. Laughter is the physiological effect of something perceived as laughable or comical. He divides it into the non-euphoric, like a polite chuckle, useful in a social context, and the euphoric laughter caused by tickling or alcohol. A curious division indeed, perhaps to indicate that one is controllable and the other is not. Anyone who is ticklish can avow that it is impossible to stop laughing however disagreeable the experience might be. This euphoric laughter can also be pathological, which reminds us of Democritus and his uncontrollable laughter. After his extensive studies, Joubert ends up stating that laughter is made up of happiness and sadness: a laughable situation gives us both pleasure and sorrow.

> Pleasure because it seems undeserving of pity, and there is no important harm or evil done, therefore the heart rejoices and swells as with real joy; there is also sorrow, since all forms of ridicule spring from something ugly and inconvenient, and the heart, thwarted in its desires, feels a sort of pain, so it contracts and shrinks.
>
> (Joubert, 2002, p. 68)

Joubert also explains melancholy – still under the influence of Hippocrates' theory of humours – as an abundance of the melancholic humour which he classifies as "scum of the blood". Mania arises when this humour is burned: this state is also called madness. Therefore, among the melancholy some laugh all the time and others weep. But certainly, of all melancholics, those whose deliriums turn to laughter are easier to than those who remain serious.

In 1648, Baltasar Gracián, a Jesuit from Aragon, Spain wrote an amazing text: *The Art and Ingenuity of Wit*, a detailed study of the possible forms of wit and its principal meaning that demonstrates how wit coins concepts through ingenuity (1996, p. 8). A first sketch of the concept of wit is presented, which is its link with the truth. But Gracián goes even further: the particularity of wit lies in its form, which is necessarily beautiful: *wit is not content with merely telling the truth, but it also aspires to beauty* (p. 32).

According to Jakob Burkhardt (1818–1897) in his book *Culture in the Italian Renaissance* published in 1860, mockery and sarcasm were the weapons to counteract the ideas of glory, the thirst for fame and extreme individualism, which were very common in this period. He describes how in the Middle Ages enemy princes and armies were provoked by sarcasm, turning its ingenuity into a weapon. He adds that wit could only become an element independent of life with the existence of its regular victim: an individual with personal aspirations. Burkhardt makes a distinction between different forms of ingenuity; the inventor of banter emerges in this period and is far superior to the court buffoon. The first aspect to appear is the comical, and when the joke is missing – called the result of contrast – there appears undisguised insolence, vulgar fraud or blasphemy and filth. He says some forms of mockery are highly comical while others are only a demonstration of presumed superiority, to defeat an adversary. In the above context, it was easy to stumble into much duress and malignity devoid of any ingenuity or wit, which must have been very disturbing for Florentine life in the Renaissance period (1999, pp. 85–87).

At this point, it is important to stop and turn to *the* great novel of Spanish literature: *The Ingenious Gentleman Don Quixote of La Mancha*. For many, *Don Quixote* is the most ingenious and entertaining book ever written. Lord Byron said that *the pleasure of reading Don Quixote in its original language outweighs all other pleasures* (Cervantes, 1972, p. XV).

We know that Freud learned Spanish so as to read this work in the original. What is more, in the correspondence that he had with his friend Eduard Silberstein, they called themselves Cipión and Berganza like the dogs in the novel *Colloquium of the Dogs* also by Cervantes. He writes to his then fiancée Martha Barnays about this epistolary period:

> We were united at a moment when friendship was not considered a sport or an advantage, but rather a necessity for a friend to live with. Really, after all the hours we spent on the school benches we have never been separated. Together we learned Spanish, we had our own mythology and our secret names taken from a dialogue of the great Cervantes [...] Together we formed a strange society of knowledge: The Castilian Academy.
>
> (E. Freud, 2006, p. 67)

The same as Rabelais, Cervantes appeared at the end of an era, in which the sacred figures of Chivalry had lost their position of ideals. Thus the labour of Don Quixote was:

> to verify for the reader that the sacred ideals of Chivalry have declined and that in reality, the ridiculous element is not his armour or his hallucinations, but rather the survival of a rhetoric peopled with majestic figures calling themselves Knights Errant.
>
> (G. Díaz & C. Brück, 1988, p.12)

In England, around the year 1600, touches of humour excite the sense of the ridiculous and make fun of that same ridiculousness. As it appears in Shakespeare's *The Merry Wives of Windsor*, the Welsh priest tells the Gallic doctor: "I beg you not to make us the object of ridicule for the humour of others" (Pollock, 2003, p. 81). In other words, there is still a remainder of the humoral theory, but when it's brought together with the mockery of what can be ridiculous, it brings a new meaning to the word humour.

In 1599, Ben Jonson defined a humourist as a funny, festive, jovial and joking person (Pollock, 2003, p. 47). From this point of view, it should be possible to become aware of the effect of humour (laughter) and to cultivate it consciously. As Asper, the protagonist of – by Jonson himself – would say:

*Now, gentlemen, I go*
*To turn an actor, and a humorist,*
*Where, ere I do resume my present person,*
*We hope to make the circles of your eyes*
*Flow with distilled laughter*

Thus, Pollock (2003) highlighted how, instead of suffering because of his moods, the humourist seeks to apply that power to his own acting ability, to produce an effect on the moods of others (p. 47). In other words, it is an action on oneself or on others. Humour, then, is a doing, but effectively a doing on oneself that can generate something in others (this will be Freud's line to be reviewed in Chapter 2).

For Pollock (2003), humour escapes any fixed determination, it rises from the depths of the body to emerge on the surface and it makes its way from medical discourse to lend itself to popular verbal puns. This is fundamental because for the first time it is used as a verb. Thus the term humour for the English, when related to the laughable, will not appear as a noun but as a verb: *to* humour.

F. Toda claimed in 1740, that there is a major moment of the English novel "sponsored" by the Licensing Act written in 1737, by which the theatre was subjected to strong political censorship. It is in this period that English literature sees the birth of the first two volumes of *The Life and Opinions of Tristram Shandy*, a gentleman in 1759 under the pen of Laurence Stern. This author – clearly influenced by the readings of Cervantes and Rabelais, as well as his contemporary J. Swift – invents a narrative with puns, *double entendres*... and that provocation to the reader to think badly and get it right.

# Modernity

Octavio Paz, Mexican writer and poet, considered *humour as an invention of the modern spirit*. We do not know whether this is true, although we can think that humour is possible in the context of a flexible axiology. The same happens with psychoanalysis, which is knowledge that is constantly being questioned. Psychoanalysis did not catch on with the medical community in Vienna. On the contrary, they refused to use the method. The first to adopt Psychoanalysis with real enthusiasm were the French surrealists who, fascinated and intrigued by Freud's *The Interpretation of Dreams*, dedicated considerable efforts to the study and dissemination of the subject. And what media can be more flexible, they thought, than art? One may deduce that there is something modern in common to both art and Psychoanalysis.

Freud had a great sense of humour in spite of the solemn image we have of him in photographs. His book *Jokes and their Relation to the Subconscious* contains a wide repertoire of jokes collected over many years. Among his favourites were those of H. Heine and his tales of Jewish people. One should mention that these short anecdotes and/or jokes convey an important part of Jewish traditions and spirit. As Theodore Reik (1994) said in *The Psychology of Jewish Humour*, "mockery usurps the seat of tragedy". The domains of comedy are as vast as those of tragedy, and in Jewish humour they are even more vast because they even embrace despair and catastrophe. *Where once there was lamentation, today there is laughter.* In the case of Jewish humour, the stories have a certain continuity and constancy. They maintain the same character throughout the centuries and are not limited by different social and cultural levels. One of the favourite targets of Jewish jokes is the military (structure), so that when an officer asks the new recruit Isaac Katzenstein: "Why should a soldier sacrifice his life for his country?" the soldier replies: "You are quite right Lieutenant, why should he?" (1994, p. 29).

In transcendental matters such as death and the relation with God, Jewish humour is particularly interesting. Many Jewish stories are tragic comedies in their relationship with this unknown deity who is always demanding personal sacrifice and renunciation, only offering promises of doubtful fulfilment in return (p. 62).

When the French Jewish writer Tristan Bernard was asked his opinion of life after death, he replied: "In the matter of climate, I would choose heaven (*le ciel*), but as for the company, I would prefer hell". There are a large number of these sayings that show a humorous relationship with God and with the possibility of a life beyond the grave.

In Mexico, there also exists a very peculiar humorous tradition in relation to death. According to André Breton, Mexico is the chosen country for black humour with its *splendid funereal toys* (1991, p. 11). He considered that the foremost genius in the realm of black humour was the plastic artist and craftsman José Guadalupe Posada for his wood carvings which lead to the awareness of the revolutionary agitation in 1910. Nothing equals the Mexican's curious relationship with death. We can find prints of a Mexican dancing with "her" (Death being female). Who can dance with Death and find it amusing?

Finally, the question about how humour works has been shown to be a necessity, since man has the possibility to live with it and re-invent himself through humour.

Humour or something related to it was undoubtedly at the dawn of the Renaissance with the great novels of Cervantes, Rabelais and with the theatre of Shakespeare and Molière, although, as shown in this chapter, it was always present in another way in philosophy or literature. Authors with sharp wit and talent were not abundant, but throughout the years, new great writers have emerged and their number slowly raised. We can find them in France, England, Germany, Argentina, Mexico and many more places. Some of their names are well known, such as Voltaire, Diderot, Artaud, A. France, Swift, Wilde, Chesterton, Heine, Borges, Paz… Humour is increasingly appreciated and is included in modern genres such as cinema: the Marx Brothers, Chaplin, Woody Allen… the list goes on.

A decade ago (2010s), I would have thought that humour will continue as long as mankind can leave his conscience behind, to travel. However, there is a new phenomenon approaching: the cancel culture.

What started as a movement to ensure the inclusion of minorities, a progressive language is becoming a witch hunt, that polarises our world. The future of humour in this context is twofold: it can be cancelled because considered dangerous or risky or it can be a way to soften our mindframes and recover diversity even when in disagreement.

# Notes

1 Plato defined man as an animal with two feet and without feathers, Diogenes liked the definition so he took a cockerel, plucked its feathers and threw it into Plato's school, saying "This is Plato's man" – D. Laercio, Vida de los Filósofos Más Ilustres, op. cit.,p. 191.
2 While taking the sun at Cranion, Alexander drew near and said to him "ask me for anything you want" upon which he replied "don't cast your shadow on me" D. Laercio, Vida de los Filósofos Más Ilustres, op. cit. p. 191.

# 2    What is humour?

There is little clarity as to what the definition of humour is, what is humorous or what "to be in a good humour" really is. In a text that proposes to use humour in psychoanalysis, psychotherapy and coaching supervision, the distinction between these three questions is indispensable. What I wish to share in the following pages, perhaps in a schematic way, required the conscientious revision of several authors in various fields. The prospect is that the effort would help to reconfigure how professionally work with humour.

To start with, we encounter various difficulties when attempting to define humour. Among them, the first seems to be that everyone thinks he knows what he is talking about when we talk of humour and, the second is that humour not only resists being defined, as Chesterton says, but also, in a certain manner, it prides itself on being undefinable; and it is generally considered a lack of a sense of humour to define it (Chesterton, 2006, p. 168). In literature, humour covers a diffuse and undefined area with so few coincidences that it would seem to be a matter of personal taste.  For the purpose of this book there is a need to define its differences clearly, so as to understand when one can use humour, when it is an invasion of the discourse of the other or when it is a social celebration just about being alive. That is to say, both humour and what is humorous play a brilliant and enjoyable role, but there is also a dark side about which it is necessary to talk to be able to distinguish it and, at times, avoid it.

As it is very attractive thanks to its effects on one's state of mind, humour is an area that has been considered in psychology, psychoanalysis, literature, philosophy and even medicine; hence there are a myriad focuses that allow us to construct a path to define it.

DOI: 10.4324/9781003154310-3

In psychology, we find that for Martin and Ford, authors of *Psychology of Humor*, humour is a form of social game "elicited by a perception of playful incongruity that produces the emotional response of mirth expressed through smiling and laughter". In the same way, for J. Gibson, humour consists in a playful use of incongruity, a positive world, as well as including various social aspects of humour such as behaviour that makes others smile, a social activity, a physiological response and even a tool for moments of stress.

For these authors, incongruity is the essential element of humour, that explains the mechanism and the understanding of humour. The social element in the ambits in which it occurs, allows us to understand in which contexts the use of humour can be important in the helping professions.

Importantly, the sense that I propose giving to humour goes much further than what causes laughter or raises a smile, as this would limit it to what I would suggest to call humorous. When you start to realise that not everything that makes you laugh or at least elicits a smile is humorous to everyone, is when you begin to differentiate the types of humour.

In the case of humour, there is a depth that we may not always recognise, perhaps because of its proximity. Just as often we do not appreciate the beauty of something because we are too close to it. For this reason, I shall begin by drawing on the vision of some poets and philosophers, who found in humour some of the most sublime expressions of the human soul.

André Bretón considers humour is the highest circle of comedy since by virtue of its tragic phase, it becomes reconciled with pain whose desperation (...) it prefers to make abstraction (p. 168). In the same way, Sören Kierkegaard reiterates that he considers humour to be "the highest circle of comedy because, in its tragic phase, it becomes reconciled with the pain whose despair (...) prefers to become an abstraction" (Pollock, 2003 p. 87).

Both authors coincide in that: (a) humour arises at a tragic or at least a painful moment, and this we encounter many times in our lives, (b) humour allows us to relate to others in a different way in a bitter moment, this consists exactly in a reconciliation at a different encounter with the same event (or person), and (c) it allows one to distance oneself from that painful place as if detaching from it, as if it were not happening to the subject.

Thus it begins to appear that humour is something to do with oneself, a mechanism that is activated inside the self. It is not something related to the surrounding environment, it is not the outside world that makes us laugh.

Psychoanalysis closely follows the lines of these inspiring views regarding humour. Freud in 1927 wrote an essay on humour and he considered it was the highest mechanism of defence, which, unlike repression, does not fall within the category of automated defence (Freud, 1080, p. 1166). The mechanisms of defence are those that the mind uses to save itself from pain, they are an automatic response, perhaps the rejection of reality itself or the pain caused by that reality. Humour appears as something very different, it does not fall into the immediate response of denial or rejection, but requires a special internal process.

E. Kris goes much further in his appreciation after innumerable hours working with patients and considers that humour is the only comic phenomenon bordering on the sublime, as it leads the patient to relate to the self (1964, pp. 30–31).

Poland describes a type of mature humour that expresses the ability to accept internal conflict and at the same time be aware of this conflict. Even if it implies limits to one's own narcissism, a sense of humour or ingenuity cannot be considered mature in itself. What determines the type of humour is its sense and its uses within the individual's psyche, not its exterior form (Poland, 1990, p. 168). That is to say, humour is part of the relationship with the self, to accept the complexity of life and to deal with it.

For Giovacchini (1991), humour can be considered as a human attribute that includes the way of perceiving the world and an attitude about the relation between the inner world of the mind and the *milieu*. Humour requires an acceptance of the reality that can be painful because of the conflict it causes in the person, whether it causes dislike, is a nuisance or is painful. He also adds that it has the elements of the primary and secondary processes, as well as creativity (p. 91). Creativity is an essential element, just accepting reality does not mean that one can deal with things with humour; this is merely the first step, there is the ingenious step of creativity that allows for the creation of a new idea and allows one to cast off the painful effect. Humour has flashes of genius.

# Why does humour matter?

Freud (1980) wrote in 1927 *Humour,* in which he states that beyond obtaining pleasure and economizing on psychic effort, humour keeps grandiose and exalted traces, thanks to which the self-triumphs over the adversity of the real circumstances of life. We can accept that life is not easy at certain moments, humour helps us overcome them as it can avert the half-bitter feeling and even draw pleasure from them. How does this triumph of the self-come about? Well, it is a demonstration of how the self is not afraid of the painful experiences in life, moreover, these life experiences can even become a source of pleasure. Humour is a para-doxical subject because it is a vehicle to obtain pleasure in spite of the painful effects that confront one and it appears to replace them.

We can conclude that also a distinctive feature of this highly praised and elusive humour is: humour is about oneself, hence humorous forms are at another's expense. Humour originates in the self although it can later be shared by everyone in an infectious way. For example, the pris-oner being conducted to the gallows on a Monday exclaims: A fine way to start the week! At first, there is nothing forcing the subject to say it, he might experience the triumph over reality internally, but as he shares it others can enjoy the bitter and the absurd of it. In fact, it gives pleasure to the person who adopts it whether there are a witness to it or not. So that the second person does not play an active part, he only benefits and obtains pleasure which he considers analogous to that which produced the humour. Freud himself, being obliged to leave Vienna, signed, under duress from the Nazis, a declaration in which he accepted that he had been treated correctly by them. Freud's son Martin Freud completed the anecdote that Freud had added humorously "I can cordially recommend the Gestapo to everyone" (Roudinesco and Plon, 1998, p. 169).

At this point, it is necessary to take up Freud's idea to explain the elation produced by humour and that seems linked to a triumph of the self over the circumstances and hence the beginning of pleasure. This is an explicable phenomenon of a special dynamic relation between structures of the mind (for this we need to follow Freud's second topic of *id, ego* and *super-ego*). At the very moment of humour, the subject is divided and takes two positions at the same time: the ego behaves like a small child facing the vicissitudes of life, and the *super-ego* (a legacy from parental incidence) takes the parental role and smiles at the hurdle in which the child finds itself, abandoning the strict vigilance (conscious or unconscious) he keeps over the ego. In this way, the super-ego sees the minor worries of the ego reduced and can contain its anguish.

Let us pause and think how this trait in the super-ego is dealt with. Humour leads us to re-think Freud in the place of the super-ego which had been considered as the "self and the other", containing indications as to how things should be in an imperative tone. This super-ego is so severe that many authors propose that one of the most significant signs of progress of the therapeutic treatment is the reduction in the demands of the super-ego so that the self can have more space to do things in life. With the advent of humour, we could think structurally about the super-ego, less strict and cruel, more permissive, where the loving rela-tionship with parents is reinstated, as if the history of the individual could be re-written. In fact in the helping professions, there is an opportunity to re-write aspects of life.

Hence, humour has the special feature of producing pleasure at the cost of repressed affection (Freud, 1980, p. 1162). Humour saves us from falling into the paralysing state of pain, it is like knowing that the pain is there but having the option of shaking it off somehow.

The possibility of humour is a reflection of a deeper relation with one's self and with the world. It is the result of a process of growth, but not an evolutionary result, rather an important change between the world and the self, which is finally the space where life happens.

However, there are other comic forms that we need to define in order to define the field of the use of humour.

## The field of comicity or humorous situations

Laughter is the effect of something humorous or comic. As Bergmann says "Only humans can laugh at ourselves, laughter is centred in humanity [...] As therapists, we should make use of this ability and make sure it is not lost" (1999, p. 28).

There are many types of laughter: from relief or joy to cruel, sadistic and sardonic, charged with aggression and sexuality. But this is not what we want to understand about humour because laughter has to do with the receiver, and since it is more connected to the ability to be able to laugh at oneself, and one's situation in the world, we want to focus on the humour of the producer. So, when we get into details one can generalise that there are different grades/levels and types of humour, that can easily be distinguished because some are more subtle than others and they are not all aggressive. So as to discern what is related to joy and what to aggression, we need to unravel what is comic, which is the simplest base of what is humorous and then go on to other more refined forms. It is important to mention these forms, as general knowledge – although only a few – is applicable in the field of the helping professions, as we shall see further on.

Kris (1964) marked the difference between what is comic and what causes laughter, he even goes a step further to say that laughter is not necessarily related to something comical. For example, children's laughter when they are playing or the laughter of a drunkard is not always caused by the perception of something comic (p. 159). Comicity entails something more than laughter. We often express our pleasure at humour, not by laughing but with a simple smile.

The forms of humour that we will be reviewing are the following:

- Comicity
- Caricature
- Parody
- Ingenuity
- Comedy
- Wit
- Irony
- Sarcasm
- Jokes

To talk of **comicity** we must resort to Henry Bergson and his classic text *Laughter*. This author describes **comicity** as something essentially human, outside this there is nothing comic (Bergson, 1939, p. 12). For example, a landscape can be ugly or beautiful, but it cannot be comical. If there were something comic it would be the part a human imprinted on it, a bridge not leading anywhere, an abandoned signboard, a door opening onto a blank wall these images remind us that laughter is centered in humanity as Bergman suggested.

The initial structures of comicity are the automatism (repetition) and rigidity of some forms or manners of the character, spirit or body (Bergson, 1939, p. 22). The rigidity of certain gestures or their repetition turns them into a stereotype and the essence to make them possible to be imitated. If someone can imitate us, it is because they have found those traits that we repeat and which are characteristic of us. Children have a great capacity for imitating adults because they observe them in great detail. This rigidity is the mechanical traced upon the living, it is a *rigidity applied to the mobility of life, a rigidity that tests the clumsiness of following the life lines and imitating their flexibility* (Bergson, 1939, p. 36). Then, Bergson defines as comic *all arrangement of acts and events that, when fitted together, give the illusion of life and a clear sensation of mechanical enchantment*, perhaps thinking that trying to imitate reality with clumsy movements would cause humour, for example, marionettes or the clockwork toys at the beginning of the 20th century.

A figure is comical when he does not seem to know that about himself (Bergson, 1939, p. 21). When the comic person is not aware of his comicity; their stereotyped traits evoke laughter and are visible to the rest of the world but invisible to themselves. This is why a ridiculous individual, from the moment he realises this, tries to disguise it or at least does his best to modify it. We can find a sort of continuity in forms of humour that goes from the comic nonsense of clowns to the most refined games of comedy. Included among them: caricature and parody. Here, the context is everything to evaluate whether the humour is denigrating the other or not. Laughing at someone who doesn't realise he is being ridiculous is charged with aggression and a lack of empathy; however, in a comedy this is the effect that is looked after: to ridicule the antagonist by means of automatised gestures about which he is unaware. Gray and Ford (2013) found that men found sexist jokes funny when told by a stand-up comedian, but they were not funny when they were told, for example, about a colleague in the workplace (p. 76). Even among a group of friends, but not so much nowadays as it would be considered politically incorrect. This form of humour is totally disallowed for the helping professions.

**Caricature** consists in exaggerating shape or features, such as setting a grimace, a pout or a sneer on a face (Kris, 1964, p. 10). For example, a caricaturist can alter the size of a nose, respecting its shape, but by lengthening it he makes a fixed expression, which is also present in the original model. Kris suggests we study the problem of comicity starting from an analysis of the caricature: its significance, history and its relation to the primary process. *Caricare* in Italian means to carry or overload with distinctive features. Thus a human face can be overloaded with its own characteristics. In addition, a caricature has an aggressive nature. It tries to find a similarity in deformity, in this way it approaches the truth more than reality itself, exposing another personality (p. 12). There is the political caricature or also in an open public square where the pavement artist invites the passer by to have his portrait drawn, no doubt they will exaggerate any defect or trait. At present, the workplace is an inexhaustible source of caricatures, such as, for example, the comic strip called Dilbert by Scott Adams. In the case of the latter, there is a relief involved in making a caricature as a result of the release of aggressiveness. There is an element of a certain comic effect present in any caricature, and it is determined partly by a feature that exposes a whole collection of disparate, boring events.

**Parody** is another field of humour, which consists of certain gestures and movements that have a comic effect (or Pantomime according to Freud). Here, the attitudes, gestures and movements of a human body can be comic as long as that body makes us think of a simple mechanism. Therefore, imitating someone means extracting part of the automatism of the person imitated and the imitator performing this mechanism with his body. For example, the gestures of an orator, which in themselves are ridiculous, inspire laughter through repetition (Bergson, 1939, p. 33). Pantomime is the comicity of movements aiming to cause laughter (like clowns), where laughter is a reaction to disproportionate gestures, in relation to what we ourselves would make in that same activity (Freud, 1980, p. 1137). Parody contains a lot of pantomime. It is interesting that the movements of a child throwing a tantrum, however, energetic and disproportionate they may be, do not make us laugh (particularly if they are ours or we are in charge of them, or we have to tolerate them in a social gathering), because this is not an intentional gesture, although it might seem artificial, actually it stems from a body deformed by anguish or fury. This is a much-used recourse in stand-up comedy or in children's theatre plays. For example, the villain of these plays is usually ridicule for his rigid, larger than life repetitive gestures, the protagonist nearly always anticipates his steps and even the way he moves. This resource allows the children to watch the action without feeling any anxiety about the villain. Here, we can see how laughter can kill fear.

Something comic appears we make when an unexpected discovery about a person. When we consider their movements, forms, acts and characteristic traits we see at first only their physical features, then their moral qualities and finally, what these movements tell us (Freud, 1980, p. 1132). There is also the comicity of situations in the same way that Bergson recreates a comic situation by making a person comical as with disguise, imitation, caricature, parody, etc. In the theatre, this form of comedy is very evident. For example, the character of *The Miser* by Molière is always making fussy gestures and exaggerated movements, which accentuate his miserliness. His companions in the play also make fussy movements that underline the comicity of the phrases or actions. In real life, one should note that this can also lead to aggressive or hostile gestures, where a person can appear without dignity or deserving respect. For instance, in schools or in meetings in the workplace, when someone imitates a person who is involuntarily comic, either by involuntary repetition of their gestures or tics, or when an irate person complains, by imitating his gesture or facial expression, attention can be diverted from the cause of his anger and invalidate it. Again, this form of comicity is very aggressive and should be avoided in any working and social environment.

This humorous form seeks to gain the complicity of the other, as a way of extending the social link; this is why Kris calls it the "social character". This is conditioned by two factors: the approval of the other person used to justify one's own aggression and an invitation to the other to adopt the same policy of aggression or regression (1964, p. 21). Consequently, these tendentious forms of comic expression help to convince and seduce the companion and are the result underlying infantile needs to connect and adapt to adult reality. The most common vehicle is through wit.

There are important differences between humour and wit. These are so evident that they are even used as one of the reasons that we can say "it's not funny", because in an attack or mockery there can be an ingenious criticism of others, but it might be cruel and it is here where humour escapes. In contrast, in humour oneself is the object of mockery, although one may not laugh. It implies the confession of human frailty;

while wit is more a forceful intellectual exercise even if on occassions it is only about a trifle. In his essay on Humour, Chesterton (2006) makes the difference:

> wit is reason seated in the judge's chair; although the accused can also receive light sentences, the key lies in the fact that the judge is never condemned. Whereas humour always entails the idea that the humourist is at a disadvantage and finds himself trapped by the entanglements and contradictions of life. Wit is an independent judge of the other judges, whether king, admiral, military tribunal or the masses.

(pp. 164–165)

Even in the 13th century, wit was distinct from humour, it was a form of intellectual ability, of the upper classes, generally acute and cutting, intelligent without passion, which must have implied knowledge acquired from books (Sanville, 1999, p. 34).

**Ingenuity** can be considered among the forms of comicity the nearest to the joke (Freud). Ingenuity has to be produced, without our intervention, in the acts or words of others, who take the part of the second person in the joke or comic situation, and appears (or malice), says Freud, principally in children, or adults with a low level of education. In his book about the Joke, he gives the example of a theatre show with a little girl and a little boy of 10 and 12 years, respectively, before an audience of family and relatives. The play consists of the story of a couple of fisher-folks, who, because they are poor decide to separate. The farewell is tender and loving. After many years they meet again; the fisherman returns with a fortune he has made and the fisher-woman says very proudly: "I have also been busy", she opens the door to her hut and shows him 12 child-like dolls. The audience who had been watching seriously and silently, suddenly burst out laughing much to the surprise of the children. Freud considers this childhood innocence to be the essence of ingenuity (p. 1134).

Ingenuity (verbal) coincides with the Joke in the expression and in the content, making a wrong use of the words, an absurdity or "dirty" joke. But the psychic process is made in the first person. The ingenuous person believes that he has made normal use of his expressive and intellectual faculties. He has not a minor second intention, nor does he get any pleasure at producing anything ingenuous (p. 1134). Whereas on the receptor ingenuity acts like a joke because it makes any censorship disappear.

The case of **Comedy** requires a more complex mixture of several elements already mentioned. To turn a theatre play into a comedy requires actions – like those of a clown – gestures that refer to the caricature – and repetition – which shows the automatism. Also constantly repeating a word or scene, the symmetrical inversion of roles and the geometric development of misunderstandings (Bergson, 1939, p. 35). One should add that the real challenge of comedy is to make it seem plausible because plausibility gives it force.

In comedy, what functions is the unmasking. Specifically, when there is someone who has been vested with authority and dignity by deceit and is subsequently exposed (for example *Les Précieuses Ridicules or Les Femmes Savantes* by Molière). Freud considered that another form of unmasking is when it happens by degrading the dignity of a person by showing his human weakness (Freud, 1980, p. 1145). The great number of television series dedicated to comedy testifies to the great affinity the human being has for this genre of entertainment. The principle of an un-masking is the same in many of them. Let us think of a comedy such as *The Office* that develops in the context of the workplace. The moments when a laugh escapes are when a culture or social habit is unmasked, the cult of the leader, a stereotype of a colleague at work, etc. In this sense, the comedy could be a form of denouncement, not necessarily a political subject, but rather to exhibit the absurdity of life in the way the characters in *Seinfeld's* comedies do. This focus, which cannot really be called existentialist, shows up the trivialities of life, the absurdities, for instance, of making plans, the blindness towards one's own situations and the cynicism resulting in the response to some of them. These are among other situations that comedy can target, but always about stereotyped characters that show the traits of most people in the post-industrial revolutionary world.

**Irony** is something really sophisticated. To begin with, it is a rhetorical figure: a form of discourse. It consists in saying something in a manner and intonation that leaves no doubt as to the true meaning, which is the absolute opposite. At present, irony can be considered, incisive, aggressive, corrosive, cruel, scathing or even sarcastic. Throughout history the meaning of irony has changed, the Greek verb *eironeomai*, signifies to conceal or hide something. Whoever uses irony (*eroneia*) says much less than he is thinking. The change lies in the fact that it has stopped being an expression in philosophical thinking and has come into general use but more as a self-indulgence as we will explain below.

There are two concepts of irony: the classic and the romantic. The classic is principally represented by Socrates. He used this resource to pretend he didn't know enough about any subject: the opponent would then manifest his opinion which Socrates would proceed to tear to pieces. By this feigned ignorance, Socrates made his opponent realise his own ignorance. So that, he who pretended not to know, did know, and he who claimed he knew, showed that he didn't. By using this resource of ignorance he made a good many enemies, since official knowledge – or the knowledgeable official – doesn't like to find himself questioned (Ferreter Mora, 1994, pp. 1903–1905), even if it is a way to obtain a new piece of knowledge. Aristotle claimed that irony counteracted boastfulness, but doesn't consider it modesty, rather a false modesty, and this is where we can place present-day connotations of irony. Aristotle's rigorous meaning made an important turn in the use of irony and, given that scholars have followed him closely, it remained over time. That this was so is shown when nearly 1,500 years later Saint Thomas considers irony to be a subtle vanity. Lacan considers that irony, far from being an aggressive reaction (by nature), is *principally a form of interrogation, a sort of question* (1994, p. 32). For Bergson irony arises when *one simply states what something ought to be, pretending that it is really so, differing from humour which is a detailed description of reality, feigning to believe that things should be so. Thus defined humour would be the reverse of irony* (Bergson, 1939, p. 97).

Turning to Romantic irony, this appears in the German writers such as Schlegel and Ferdinand Solger, the common concept of irony is to present this as a union of contrasting elements such as Nature and Spirit, the objective and the subjective, etc.

**Sarcasm** can be defined as a mockery, or irony that insults, despises, humiliates or cruelly ridicules someone. It is an openly sadistic manifestation towards the other, as much as sadism is the sexual perversion where the satisfaction is linked to the suffering of and the humiliation inflicted on the other. Psychoanalysis has demonstrated how sadism takes many forms and is a component of sexual life, and when it appears in an adult it is considered as the manifestation of traces of infantile sexuality. For Reik, one can talk about cordial irony, but not cordial sarcasm because sarcasm is incisive and cutting, to the extreme of elementary impulses. Its words are also deadly. The very term sarcasm derives from a Greek word meaning lacerate or mutilate – ridicule is also deadly (Reik, 1994 p. 101). Let us think about the sarcasm that was used in schools in the middle of the last century that has been so heavily criticised. Sarcasm, by far, is the humorous figure most to be avoided in sessions, because generally there is a victim and a victimizer. It is a form of relation, based on disparity that allows bullying or the abuse of authority. Although it is used widely in normal life, in the scripts for television and cinema and in comedy shows, its use in sessions can be lethal in a profession where the patient or client requires special care because of the phenomena of transference and confidence that exist.

Since we have seen how the different forms of comicity have evolved throughout history, in this work we have not yet looked at the Joke, which is one of the principal formations of the unconscious mind which Freud wrote extensively and it is probably one of the handiest resources to use in coaching supervision.

> Just as watches are placed in precious cases to encase their most excellent machinery, so often it happens with a joke: its best products of its creation are used to enclose the most valuable thoughts.
>
> (Freud, 1980, p. 1078)

Jokes and humour are not the same thing. Many discussions related to the use of humour in several situations (including sessions of analysis) would be shortened if these two genres were not confused. In the bibliography studied the joke is one more example of the humoristic catalogue.

Freud wrote a well-known book, but not much worked with, *The Joke and its Relation to the Unconscious* in 1905 (Roudinesco and Plon, 1998, p. 11). A common criticism of this text is that it is boring or dense; there is the fantasy that to think of a book about the joke must be amusing or humorous, why should it be so? Of course, the book by Freud is interesting but not funny in spite of containing some good anecdotes and jokes. It is like analysing a joke, it immediately stops being funny when one tries to explain it. The same happens with detective stories. While the intrigue develops for Mrs. Marple, Holmes or Poirot the reader is captivated by the story, but once the mystery is solved, the story ends, there is no longer any interest. This happens with a joke. When one inspects the mechanisms that make it work it loses its funny side, nevertheless it is a necessary task.

The literature about the Joke in psychology is so scarce that this is possibly the reason that Laplanche and Pontalis do not include an entry for Joke nor for Witz in their dictionary of Psychoanalysis. It is Lacan who takes up the interest in this work in his essay *"The instance of the word in the unconscious"* (1958) classifying Freud's text as canonical; in addition, he made a study of Witz in his seminar V: *The formations of the subconscious,* carried out that same year.

In *The Joke and its Relation to the Unconscious* Freud classifies the joke as a factor of psychical power, whose intervention can be decisive (Freud, 1980, p. 1103). This does not satisfy our curiosity, since on occasions to tell a joke could be considered as evasive, to divert attention from the subject, but it is really important to read carefully what surrounds the joke. It is so revealing that it is included among the phenomena called formations of the unconscious such as symptoms, dreams, mistakes, forgetfulness, etc. A formation of the unconscious is an encounter of two opposing forces, one coming from the self – which consists in censorship – and the other that seeks expression and which comes from the unconscious, also relating to vestiges of the subject's childhood. When these force are confronted they produce something new and they release energy. A joke is pleasurable when it allows repressed material to be liberated and this produces a release of energy, which had been destined to repress said material.

This piece proposes the need to study the joke and its relation to the unconscious processes since the joke uncovers something of the truth – at least for the subject creating it, recognising beforehand the aggressive trait can derive from a joke. In the helping professions, we have to deal with reality, with truth, with is in the environment and on the interior of the individual that is our patient or client.

At first glance, we do not know what causes us pleasure in a joke or why we laugh. This seems enigmatic, and this is what draws attention to it: if a joke causes laughter it is because it has established a disposition contrary to criticism in the subject. It imposes a state of mind easily satisfied by the game (children's) which the joke has tried to replace by all strategies (Freud, 1980, p. 1103).

# Why does a joke work?

There are two main theories about how it works:

## *Motivation of the teller*

The joke provides the possibility of evading repression which implies renouncing childish libidinous impulses. A joke can be humorous as long as it allows for the release of tension.

A joke represents a rebellion against authority. Jokes have facades that can hide what they have to say and they can also hide what is forbidden for them to say. This is the paradox. The path is the casing for a watch that Freud was referring to, that keeps its precious contents forbidden, both sexual and aggressive, not quite hidden but allowing a chink, a door to the outer world, where others can see it. At present, a joke can be thought of as a way of by-passing material from the unconscious, which may not be only hostile or aggressive, but might also show pain or frustration.

Usually, a joke that causes a guffaw is tendentious and always has a double meaning to stimulate thought, strengthening it and ensuring it against criticism. We are not talking about classifying jokes into cleaner or harsher than others, it's not about wit. The main interest – as follows – is understanding the mechanism of a joke.

The processes of the technique of a joke are the same as those that make dreams: condensation, displacement and representation of contradiction. These mechanisms are unconscious and cannot be learned, not even in a sufficiently good development of the mind – with a sufficiently good mother – Winnicott would say. In therapeutic processes, analysts have managed to distinguish them amongst the material that surfaces itself before them. It would be interesting if the processes used in training supervisors for "Coaching", particularly these phenomena of displacement in the subconscious, could be studied in depth, so as to locate counter-transfer phenomena. This is, what the supervisor is feeling might be the result of displacement phenomena in the supervised subject.

The material in the unconscious of the subject includes experiences and fantasies from childhood. A joke draws on this material for its creation, it delves into the unconscious to find the old play on words/word games from the past, which allows him to take possession of this old source of pleasure (Freud, 1980, p. 1126).

If we consider that the joke follows the same mechanisms as the work of dreams, then the subject does not control his humorous productions the same as his nightmares. *An enigma is the reverse of the joke* (Freud, 1980, p. 1126).

## *Incongruity*

This theory belongs to cognitive psychology and it is about the surprise reaction when faced with incongruous events. This theory is based on the motivations of whoever tells the joke and what gains he may derive from. Martin and Ford (2018) say that we experience mirth and laughter when we notice a mismatch between our sensory perception of reality and our conceptual understanding of it.

Incongruity, then is a key element to make a joke humorous. However, it is not the only element. There is a need for incongruity to be resolved. This resolution is what makes the joke funny.

Suls proposes a two-stage model of humour appreciation in which the mechanism of humour is a problem-solving task.

> According to the model, a joke setup causes the listener to make a pre-diction about the likely outcome. When the punch line does not conform to the prediction, the listener is surprised and looks for a cognitive rule that will make the punch line follow from the material in the joke setup. When this cognitive rule is not found however, the incongruity remains, eliciting puzzlement rather than amusement. Thus, in this view, mirth results from the resolution of an unexpected or surprising incongruity, rather than from the ongoing presence of an incongruity.
>
> (Martin and Ford, p. 57)

Example:
MOTHER: "Doctor, come at once! Our baby swallowed a fountain pen!"
DOCTOR: "I´ll be right over. What are you doing in the meantime?"
MOTHER: "Using a pencil".

In this example, it is quite easy to see the two steps of the mechanism of the incongruity and the subsequent production of humour. In the first instance, when the mother asks the doctor for help and he asks about the measures the mother is taking, the mind begins to predict the range of possible answers. However, the mother says that what she is doing is using a pencil. This is the moment when the incongruity appears and the surprise at the unexpected reply. Then the listener has to go back to find the connection as to why that reply, thus solving the mystery of the surprise.

The theory of incongruity does not check to see if the jokes are sarcastic or hostile, the analysis focuses principally on showing the incongruity and the surprise at the resolutions.

Contemporary research supports the incongruity resolution theories, showing that when people are presented with humour material that contains: resolvable incongruity, they engage in two distinct cognitive processes: the incongruity detection, rapidly followed by the incongruity resolution. However, the hypothesis that amusement with all humour requires one to engage in both incongruity detection and resolution has received less support. It might be that both processes of incongruity detection and resolution are involved in deriving amusement from jokes and cartoons that present resolvable incongruity, but that resolution is not required for one to derive amusement from nonsense jokes, which do not present any resolvable incongruity.

# Differences between joke and humour

Briefly, the joke provides momentary pleasure. On the contrary, humour can manage to avoid the psychic effort that restrains what is painful, so it is a saviour. It is manifests in a moment (like the joke), but it relates to the internal psychic work done in a way that it remains permanently in the mind.

Another fundamental difference between them is the number of persons who participate in each. For example, in the joke it is necessary to have three persons: the one who tells the joke, the one who inspires the joke and the one the joke is about and who accepts it with a smile. It should be noted that the first and third persons are those who gain pleasure, but it is more manifest in the third person through laughter.

On the other hand, a joke cannot exist without the "other", it needs an audience, a witness to bear out what has been said. In humour, Freud says the listener is "only like an echo, a copy" of what happens in the humourist. This is why he considers that humour has a certain dignity lacking in the joke because the latter only serves to benefit pleasure or show aggression. For Kris humour is also sublime: it is in relation to the subject himself and does not need others in order to generate pleasure.

One last comparison between the joke and humour, and perhaps the most important one:

The joke provides a momentary gratification, whether from the production of mirth or the relief of tension, but humour implies a form of gratification beyond the painful moment. It consists of a victory of the self over the circumstances. It is the person talking to himself. It is the super-ego, coming to console the self by means of humour, just like a father consoling his son.

Several schools of psychoanalysis consider the super-ego becoming flexible as a result of the analysis. In this way, the appearance of humour (not the humorous event) in a person reveals an important change in the relation with himself, perhaps an interior dialogue, in which a person finds his own words to console himself.

The foregoing text would enable the possibility of incorporating humour within the individual's existence, in his psychotherapeutic, coaching or supervision processes. It is quite evident that the capacity for humour is not entirely existent in all people.

Along these lines, Kris considers humour as a consequence of the transformation of the subject: *humour is a precious gift, it makes men wise, then these are sublime and are sure, it draws outsiders from all conflicts* (Kris, 1964, p. 76).

Humour, then, is something that makes us human, but not because it makes us great, nor superior to other beings who inhabit this earth, but because it makes us recover in all humility from the vicissitudes of life with a smile, with an acceptance verging on wisdom. Humour is like a hand that lifts us up and invites us to go on in spite of the circumstances. Only that the hand is our own self. This is what humour makes possible.

*Humour is the son of ingenuity and joy, and the grandson of truth.*
*R. Addison.*

(Pollock, 2003, p. 78)

# 3 The awakening of humour

In Chapter 2, we established the fact that humour is a refined ability acquired through life. So the following questions are natural: How does it begin to appear? Can we talk of humour since infancy? If that is so, what begins to show in those first years? Research or theory about this "gestation" of humour is not abundant in the literature of psychoanalysis; however, some important theorists like Mahler and Anna Freud, to mention two, have pointed to certain aspects worth highlighting. Conversely, there are numerous studies in cognitive psychology dedicated to the evolutionary development of humour since the earliest infancy. Cognitive theories focus on the relative capacities of memory, language and perception, while psychoanalytical theories show the degree of development of the self and of the emotional level of the child. This is why it is necessary to run through both these theories to provide a better approximation to the question: How and when does humour develop in the human being? As a starting point, we can notice that both state similar facts regarding the importance of the relation between play and humour.

## Cognitive research into the development of humour

An important concept that functions as the guiding thread of this research is the *Theory of the Mind*, which is the capacity of the mind to recreate the intentions and points of view of others. This is done not as a divination, but rather as an inference from the words of the other. It involves a certain sympathy towards the jokes of the other, as well as in shared thoughts and/or

DOI: 10.4324/9781003154310-4

values. It is also an indicator of social links and how humour has a place in encounters with others. Social links with persons other than parents or caretakers do not appear before the age of four. This concept will appear further on to be able to understand the difference between experience and comicality, humour and even irony.

There is a moment when a smile and laughter first appear in a baby. Though it cannot be considered as the development of humour, it can be thought of as a physiological response that later will accompany the different stages of humour. Smiling can begin as early as three weeks to six months in the interactions of the infant with its parents or whoever is its principal caretaker.

Between the ages of 6 and 12 months, the game of "peek-a-boo" can begin: a familiar person constantly appearing and disappearing behind a blanket or a door in front of the baby. There is obvious pleasure in the "reappearance", shown by smiles and even laughter. In contrast, at the moments of disapperance, there is a silent expectation in which the functions of perception and recognition are fully alert. Although we cannot yet speak of humour, we can think of games, and of the disposition towards humour when this activity takes place, and we shall take this up further on. Laughter and game playing appear at similar ages and are related to context. Humour and games can also appear when the child feels safe with its parents or primary caretakers. Caregivers teach infants to recognise verbal and behavioural cues that imply the activity is a game (Martin & Ford, 2018).

Several authors (Martin & Ford, Gibson) share McGhee's theory in *The Developmental Stages of Humour* in which, from a cognitive point of view, the essence of humour is considered in the different relations the psyche has with incongruity as well as how those relations evolve throughout the development of the child. This view is profoundly influenced by the theories of Cognitive Development by Piaget (Gibson, 2019). Although there are discussions among researchers in the psychology of development, we can consider these four levels to generally describe the progress of the concept of humour within the relations of the child and the world:

1.  *Incongruous actions of objects*. This can vary, but it generally appears before the age of two and a half, when children are able to play with fantasy. Humour at this stage lies in using objects in ways that do not

correspond to them. That is to say, the game is the mismatch between the objects and their function. The child recognises that is not the function of the object, but plays with it in an incongruous way. For example, the child places its plastic mug on its ear and pretends it is a telephone. He recognises the mistake as game playing.

2. *Incongruous labelling of objects and verbal play*. For this stage, it is necessary that the child should have a certain command of the language and can play with it. This is approximately at 3 years of age. The child then plays with mismatches between the objects and their names. It is not about the child making a true mistake but rather he actively makes the change: in this way, he plays at calling his head, his "foot" or the biscuit a "soup". One can easily picture the mischievous look in the child's eyes as he tests these fake mistakes and checks their effect on his parents as they join in the game.

3. *Conceptual incongruities*. These are possible when the child's language capacity grows. When there is further understanding of the correlation between the name and the object, the object now belongs to a category of attributes with which one can play. An example is a common game where the child says that the cow goes *meow* and the cat goes *bow-wow*. At this moment, we can confirm that incongruity has already reached a conceptual level.

4. *Multiple meanings*. At about 7 years of age, humour reaches a sophisticated level that allows for irony and satire. It has now developed the Theory of Mind (the capacity to recreate in the mind the intentions and points of view of others). The child can already manage complex schemes of representations and abstractions of objects and things, as well as anticipating what the other can be thinking or feeling. At this stage, children are less egocentric and start to give greater consideration to the perspectives of those around them. These cognitive activities (the representation of things) and the capacity for empathy allow him to understand more sophisticated levels of what is humorous: that is, they allow him to make inferences about language, as well as about the intention of the person telling a joke.

One example: "Why did the old man tip-toe past the medicine cabinet?"

"Because he didn't want to wake up the sleeping pills".

According to Martin and Ford, children first need to recognise that the intention of the phrase is not what it appears to be, and then they need to substitute the true sense for the literal sense. This requires two mental steps: the first is to recognise that irony is used to disguise a criticism or praise and that in doing so it helps to tone down the intention. The second step is to recognise that the irony lies in the contrast between the literal and the intended sense and that this incongruity is the vehicle for humour. This realisation confirms the concept of a "Theory of the Mind". At first, children understand irony but do not necessarily find it humorous, but once they discover its use they can find it funny. The intonation of an ironic phrase can also have an important effect to see if the child will join in the humour and laugh. Thus, humour becomes a sort of social glue that inserts the child and the adult into their milieu and benefits his psychological disposition.

Cognitive research has focused mostly on the early years of life considering that the elementary functions for the development of humour are already established by the age of eight. Afterwards, during adolescence, the main shift is that sexual or aggressive content becomes a key component in humour, but this is an area to be dealt with more deeply by psychoanalysis. We should add that in terms of age, the older the person, the greater the affinity to irony. It should also be said that in general, the development of humour shows a slow shift, from a world more centered on the self, in which it is the child who plays the games of mistakes and is the object of the joke, to a world with greater social interaction and multiple meanings (McGhee) in which it is necessary to consider the references to words in order to recognise the implied emotions and feelings. Humour in children allows research studies as well as clinicians to gain an idea of their psychological state.

Humour, as a tool for coping, is something that has been worked on deeply in psychoanalysis and which we shall see in the following chapters.

# The development of humour from the psychoanalytical point of view

Psychological experience shows the evolutionary stages of the self and the quality of emotions in relation to the other, whether conscious or unconscious. It is thus interesting to collate the observations of psycho-analysis and cognitive psychology about the human mind and specific-ally about humour.

## From word games to humour

From the point of view of French-school psychoanalysis, there is an "entry into language" that starts at birth, even if the baby cannot pronounce any words. Dolto (2001) established that the starting point of laughter and humour is the use and abuse of word games. In her text *On the symbolic function of words (pp. 10–11)*, she describes an encounter with a baby of nine months. This takes place in a park, where she meets a woman carrying the baby in a stroller. Dolto was wearing a hat and she notices the child's interest in it, so a game starts in which she presents the object for the child to take and says "hat", and alternates it with its disappear-ance saying "no hat". As the game wears thin, she introduces a variant: she shows the hat, saying "no hat". At this point, something unexpected happens: the baby starts to laugh uncontrollably, and as long as the game is repeated, it continues to laugh.

This episode leads one to think how it can be that a child who cannot yet speak is capable of playing a word game. For Dolto (2001), this child soon perceives the contradiction between what is being said and the actual sensorial experience, *and here the intended equivocation gives a human dimension of complicity that gives value to the subjects and owners of reality*. This is where the origin of humour is to be found: in the origin of word games, *games where subjects dominate things and, by subjecting them to their symbolic function, can enjoy even the contradic-tion that confirms them* (p. 13).

In the United States during the 1950s, M. Mahler carried out research in the Master Children's Centre on the patterns of evolution of the mother–child relationship. From the birth of the child up to the consolidation of its identity as a child, she wanted to find the roots of psychosis. Based on lon-gitudinal observations of mother–child pairs, Mahler identified a normal development which she called *separation and individuation*, which covers ages from six months to three years, and which consists of four sub-phases: differentiating, exercising, approaching and achieving the constant object.

In this process, Mahler (2000) considered humour to be found in relation to the development of basic states of mind, which reminds us somewhat of the ancient Greek theories. She proposed that there is a special mood of *delight and exaltation* in the sub-phase of exercising, particularly when a child stands upright (approximately from 10 to 18 months).

Mahler says this mood manifests as a sense of "greatness, omnipotence and conquest which is almost delirious", according to the age of the infant. Mahler shows that this mood of the child, whose "walking" is now the peak of his abilities, also makes him aware of how small he is in comparison with the outside the world.

From the 15 to 18-month stage onwards, there should be a gradual recognition of the disconnect between the child's illusion of grandeur and the obstacles that make his adaptation to the realities of life so difficult. In this way, the child realises his separation from the mother: he sees himself as relatively small. He has to confront dangers as a solitary, weak individual, and those dangers seem overwhelming for his abilities. In this way, the previous mood of greatness disappears and a mood of relative calm predominates, and even temporary bouts of sadness. However, what seems to offset the *rather abrupt deflation* from the illusions of greatness and omnipotence is the weight of his motor functions, which now temper his belief in his physical strength and the pleasure he takes in its mastery (Mahler, 2000, p. 241).

Therefore, it is possible to observe how the appearance of humour can modify a sentiment of delight/omnipotence, as it now relates to the appreciation of reality in which the subject realises he is in a humble position that seems to contradict the strange sensation of greatness. Realising his fragility, he seems completely disarmed: but still, as a consequence of separation and by accepting reality, he begins to know his own body and calculate possibilities and hopes of success in his physical environment. The child measures his possibilities in relation to what his body can do; for example, to crawl to another place, to reach the armchair where the cat is, to reach the place where his mother is. Getting to know these possibilities and measuring the effort required, fills him with hope to continue trying out more things. The more things he can do, the more he wants to try.

Winnicott's perspective on the matter is that play – and later, humour – have their origins in what is called the *transitional space*. At an early stage in the baby's life, mother and child establish a very special relationship which leads to the *transitional phenomenon*. A hungry baby calls for a breast and it appears. In the mind of the baby, he has created this object that appears at his command, because he still does not realise the limits between his own body and the "outer world". When the mother responds to that call, she builds a feeling of omnipotence in the child; that is to say, she appears and the baby "creates the breast" in its mind. Later she will "disillusion" the baby when it discovers that it doesn't belong to him but to the mother and that he is an object separate from the mother, and furthermore, that there is a limitation that separates him from the outer world. But this intimate space created together does not disappear, it is a space destined for imagining, playing and creating. In adult life, it corresponds to shared spaces that can be created by phenomenons ranging from religion to art, as well as through creative work.

In order to study game playing and the cultural life of an individual, it is necessary to examine this zone called *transitional Space*, which is a period of adaptation arising from the love and trust learned from the mother.

In infancy, this intermediate zone is necessary for the child to begin to relate to the outer world and it is made possible by a good mother–child relationship in the critical early phase. However, Winnicott (1999) emphasised that acceptance of reality is never complete. That is, no human being is free of the tension caused by relating exterior reality with one's interior reality, although relief from this tension is to be found in this intermediate zone. This is the zone where we find direct continuity to the *play zone* where the small child loses itself in play (p. 322). The lack of confidence or loss of the object (mother/breast) signifies for the child the loss of his play zone, and the consequent loss of its significant symbol.

During the transitional phase, the child lives simultaneously between two worlds due to the use of humour. Humour is what allows for harmony between reality and illusion, since it introduces a point of view that can turn potentially serious situations, into situations which are no longer threatening, and even fun (Giovacchini, 1999, p. 92).

Winnicott (2002) declared it is fundamental for the analyst to recognise the existence of this transitional space between patient and analyst: the only space where the game can begin, a space of continuity and contiguity. If this playing space does not exist, the first task is to take the patient from a state where he cannot play, to one where it is possible to do so (p. 61).

Some authors go a step further and conclude that if it is possible to create a transitional space, then it is also possible to generate humour:

...In structural terms, the very act of entering or creating a transitional space also generates humour which, as a positive form of feedback, contributes to detoxing reality and replaces it with playful fantasies. This introduces a perspective for observation in which the patient and the analyst examine the patient-analyst relationship and on occassions, there will be light kidding in their dialogues in the interest of a therapeutic solution (Giovacchini, 1999, p. 9).

In contrast, Melanie Klein (2003), who was known for her profound observations and work on infants and children, states that

the primary link of the child with the breast and mother's milk constitutes the basis of all loving relationships in its life ... the breast and its product ... become symbols of love, pleasure and security in the child's mind.

(p. 328)

Based on this perspective of Klein's, Sanville (1999, p. 49), proposes an original idea for the beginning of humour. Both Klein and Sanville agree the baby does not realise at first that the "good mother", who is full of milk and good moods, is the same as "the bad mother", who has no milk and has a bad temper. Klein considers that the shifting positions of the mother and the child are the centre of what could generate humorous situations. That is, the mother, with her own actions and words, shows the child how to enjoy itself when faced with difficult situations: she shows how to generate a special sense of self, a sense of humour.

There is a psychic inequality due to the structural difference between the baby and the adult. Given that a sufficiently good mother can enjoy her baby, she can make the baby laugh at itself even before it knows what it is laughing at, which lays the ground for it to develop a sense of joy about the human condition. In this sense, the two authors show how the child can have a healthy sense of self when the mother, acting as a mirror, can approach the child with a humorous attitude. One can think of the baby's smile of satisfaction when it lets go of its mother's nipple when she has finished breastfeeding it. In this give and take, the baby can receive milk because it sucks: because it asks for it and gets it. In a session of analysis or supervision, the patient or coach experiences a "loving" listening: he goes and talks, and when he talks something is produced. That space becomes a new space for thinking together.

Sanville considers that in girls of about two years, an enormous jump can be observed in ordinary game playing, when the exchange of roles with the mother becomes manifest. For example, when the child says "now I'm going away and you will start to cry". When the little girl can think of what it feels like to be a mother and imagines the mother in the role of a daughter, what we are seeing is a play-rehearsal for the later stages of *absence* and *independence*. This is what Freud would call the development of a person through humour because this little girl can see herself as a child, but she can also play the superior role of a mother with her child (Sanville, 1999, p. 41).

Other psychoanalytic authors think of the emergence of humour along the lines of development as proposed by A. Freud (1993, p. 54). For Poland (1990), there can be a line of development of a sense of humour that runs parallel to psychosexual development and object relations.

This begins at the moment of a baby's smile of satisfaction after suckling, continuing through the sadistic pleasure of manipulating others, to the delight of playing with words – a game which helps realise one's limitations, such as guessing games or the sexually aggressive jokes and jests of adolescence. According to Poland (1990), humour comes later, which he considers as the ability to recognise urges, frustrations and hopes in a way that bitterness is mocked but not denied (2002). One should point out that this does not appear to be a "natural", continuous line, since in this proposal there is a great psychic leap – almost an abyss – between what he considers humour and the salacious jokes of adolescents. In this sense, we should remember that a joke is not necessarily humour.

Having entered the realm of language, we can talk about jokes and word games. Freud (1980) supposed a specific development of the joke, as linked to the development of the person. The joke begins as a game aimed at giving pleasure deriving from the free use of words and ideas.

Later, when the child begins to reason, and censure begins to expand its field of action, word games are rejected because they make no sense. But the self not only does want to maintain that source of pleasure but also to gain a new source: by liberating such "nonsense" as a catharsis from the tension of withholding it. Further down the line, word games turn into jests. When this jest is applied to the manipulation of ideas, their expression and their defence against critical judgement (an activity that elicits confusion about the sources of pleasure), we can start to consider it as true joking, exempt of biased intent (i.e. aggression) (p. 1106). In this way, humour fills an important role in the fight against the repression of interior obstacles, according to the theories of pleasure.

According to Freud, the joke remains true to its essence, from its origin in childhood up to its perfection in adulthood. As the primitive sources of verbal pleasure are maintained, they evolve and pass through jest and to reach other new sources, as it fights its way against repression and critical judgement.

Kris (1964) highlighted an important moment in the life of a child: the moment he understands a joke made by an adult or when he himself makes his first joke. This is only possible when he achieves mastery over judgement of "what might seem funny". For instance, an absurd movement made by another person appears funny to a child only when he has mastered that movement himself. Later, he can laugh at an error of thought when "his own powers" of thinking have been established. This indicates that the understanding of a joke or jest can only be acquired when language has been properly mastered (p. 60). Kris does not provide any suggestion about the mechanics of how this happens.

The joy found in word games survives as the pleasure that as adults they will find in words. The pleasure in the joke is explained as an experience of control of the self over the *Primary Process*, something wished for, but in another way would happen against the will of the self. This is about a passive experience that is reproduced actively (p. 62). In adults, we find these signs of joy when they join in or invent plays on words. This gives us an idea of the importance of keeping a small space and capacity for this mode of enjoyment.

For Kris, in the first phase of a child's development, game playing serves to dominate the toy/object which was previously his body. Later on, it allows for the active dramatisation of the interior world, as Freud (1980) showed in *Beyond the Beginning of Pleasure* in relation to child play. For example, when a toddler goes to the paediatrician it is generally a difficult and memorable experience. As he gets home or goes to school, he continues to play doctor, giving injections and examining his playmates' bodies. He can still be afraid of the visits, but he also experiences a pleasure that allows him to dominate his fear. Kris considers this game a real pleasure as well as a regression and a discovery, similar to the game of hide-and-seek, that a child plays over and over again.

The perception of what can be amusing is a preliminary phase to understanding what is funny, and Kris considers it an illusion that replaces reality, just as in a world of fiction things that were forbidden might become acceptable. Game playing is thus a space with expanded boundaries. For Kris, game playing is solitary, while amusement is social, and the salacious jokes of an adult have their origin in amusement. We can further add that humour has its origins in game playing.

During adolescence, the individual goes through a series of revolutions in his relations with his family and his own body. There is a struggle towards *independence* and *identity-defining* and at the same time a *separation* from parents. Adolescents find themselves in a period of indecision, searching for autonomy and independence. Dolto says that adolescence is like a birth that should not be delayed because the individual feels the absolute need to be free from the influence of the family *milieu*. Concurrently, there is a sexual awakening, with physical changes accompanied by desires and impulses towards the other, and therefore language, games and jokes become charged with sexual content. Jokes, irony and even sarcasm are used as means of expression: these forms of humour are an escape valve for the psychic problems of the adolescent. The jokes and sarcasm can be directed to a group, one person in particular – typically one of their peers – or an authority figure like teachers or parents. This outpour of aggressive and sadistic impulses makes these years very complex for adolescents and for those close to them. In the helping professions, it is very important to identify these elements in the speech of the young, thus helping them realise their relation with the world and how they are facing this complex stage of life.

## *Humour in later years*

In later stages of life, the understanding of humour diminishes in terms of cognitive capacities (Martin & Ford), but this decrease can be also understood by the loss of context that arises from the disconnect to new language or new lifestyles. Nevertheless, the pleasure experienced with humour can in fact be even greater, because with the passage of time one may acquire "wisdom" (although there are no guarantees!).

Kohut (1969) related humour to wisdom and defines the latter as the sum of a sense of humour, the acceptance of the fact that life is finite, and the acceptance of a system of acquired values which have been weighed and reflected upon throughout one's existence.

> In contrast with an attitude of utter seriousness and solemnity *vis-à-vis* the approaching end of life, the truly wise are able to transform the mood of their years of maturity into a sense of proportion, with a touch of irony towards the achievements of individual existence, including even their own wisdom.
>
> (pp. 243–272)

*Exit Laughing, How humour takes the sting out of death*, is a compilation in which 24 essayists write personal stories about how they were able to find humour in the face of death. In this account, V. Zackheim (2012) stated that "in fact, one should ask oneself if the recognition and assumption that life comes to an end is only possible after a profound exercise that starts with humour".

Both cognitive and psychoanalytical theories concur that humour rarely appears at an early age. What appears in infancy are only its first hints: games, smiles and shared happiness, but one cannot yet say that it is "a victory over defeat", as was discussed in Chapter 2. What can be said is that certain traits of humour appear in different stages of development, but that it might not appear in its maturity until one can look at oneself with both benevolence and patience, and accepting one's own defects.

# 4

# Humour during sessions

In recent years, discussions have increased concerning the use of humour in sessions of psychotherapy and psychoanalysis, but above all, regarding persons who would be in favour of a practice that could include it within a determined methodology. Although there are many similarities in the different fields, what follows are some theoretical proposals that could be applied in psychotherapy, on the one hand, and in psychoanalysis on the other hand.

## Humour in the helping professions

In the field of the psychology of humour, there are extensive studies to determine its impact on physiological aspects of the body, on the feeling of well-being, in the development of humour over time, on the capacity of producing and appreciating humour at moments of stress, in the differences in humour at different ages, etc. This shows that there is a great deal of measurable information about humour. Since the 1960s, this subject has been a task of much interest to experimental psychology. In spite of this, there is less information regarding interventions during sessions. How is humour considered in therapy? What resources are there? How to apply this, when in theory it is considered that humour is a serious incongruity? In the following chapters, we shall attempt to answer these questions.

DOI: 10.4324/9781003154310-5

## Paradoxical intention

There is no specific methodology for the use of humour *per se,* but there are methodologies that use forms of humour, considering incongruity in the paradoxical intention. Riebel (1984) carried out an extensive research on this line of therapy in which, as from 1960, the therapist, instead of joining the patient to go against the symptom seems to ask him to expand it, to explore or continue it, but not challenge it. Following we shall share some of the most relevant experiences of Riebel's thorough study:

1.  The first to propose the paradoxical intention as a technique was Victor Frankl. Since then it has been used in therapies for various purposes, in the treatment of phobias and obsessions, schizophrenia, help rejection, family fights, anorexia and compulsive eating, among others.
2.  The paradox is also used as a tool within the Interactual view. The paradox consists in sending a message that has two different levels, one which qualifies and contradicts the other. It is a message that puts the patient in conflict and that can only be resolved by giving up the problem, e.g., keep having your problem or increasing it. The sentence can cause humour because of the incongruity, but also allows for the choice of two conflicts. The first is to decide to continue the process of psychotherapy and the other is to opt for plunging into the conflict, which no doubt is limiting for life. Moreover, the choice will help to diminish the resistance to the symptom. The implicit message is that there is a problem, a pain that is already there and it is not going away.
3.  Eriksson also shares the use of the paradox for what he calls the double blind as a tactic within his therapeutic practice. Again, there is the question of whose options are directed towards curing the patient, but allow him the illusion of choosing, for example: would you prefer to start with symptom A or with symptom B? The answer implies that the patient agrees to work on one of them. A question that could cause a surprise and, therefore be near to humour, would be: do you want to be cured on a Wednesday or would on a Thursday do? Basically, there is no possible cure for a certain day, however, the patient is accepting the premise that there is a cure.

4. The paradigmatic psychotherapy sets out a number of solutions to a series of problems and resistances so as to develop insights. This therapy – more than the humour – enters the field of play, as the therapist assumes different roles of the patient's ego; while being "mirrored" can see himself, sometimes fearfully, sometimes with laughter and sometimes with relief. Performing that part of the ego is to join the symptom and expose it. This therapy has been recommended for borderline patients, paranoids and masochists; it has also proved effective with adolescents.

5. Selvini has considered the paradox as a way to break with the fundamental rule of the patients with anorexia. In this condition, the patient is usually part of a family system that is generally rigid and the symptom is only a way of escaping from it. So Selvini shares a case where paradoxically the psychotherapist gives a directive (temporary) to continue without eating as a form of unbalancing the system that forces the patient to eat and also allies himself with the patient. In the end, Selvini says, this instruction by the therapist can only win, since he will gain the confidence of the patient so as to form a strong therapeutic alliance or perhaps propitiate the disobedience to the instruction by this gaining the objective of getting the patient to eat.

6. There is also the paradoxically benevolent look at the symptom, by means of which the proposal is to treat it as an ally – or a friend – such as suggested by Weeks and Labate. That is to say, a place to combat the symptom and to try to work against it. The idea is to consider it an element arising from the past, or rather that the psyche's needs are today to carry out a specific function for the self. In this way, there is a dialectic way to dialogue with the symptom instead of having to defend himself from it.

7. In the hyperbolic therapy proposed by Grossman the therapist validated the irrational side of the patient; in a way that the patient no longer feels the need to defend himself from the symptom, the more irrational the better. Carried out correctly, it is possible that the option whose material was not present will appear for the therapeutic work. Again, it is the incongruence that leads to the resolution. If the patient says something irrational – because he usually knows that it is and in most situations, he will have to defend it – the therapist responds

with something quite unexpected, as if he were in strong alliance with him. This way could generate either confidence or surprise, both results being fruitful in the therapeutic process.

Harvey Mindess is a clinical psychologist who shares his experience in the practice of humour in sessions, with the assurance of the doubtful. In his book *The Use of Humour in Psychotherapy*, he starts by recognising that although many clinicians doubt the effectiveness of humour in psychotherapy, he is basically one of them, it does not prevent him from attempting to write about it. Mindess includes among the ways of using humour in psychotherapy: (1) telling jokes related to the dilemmas the patients are going through, (2) reinforcing the attempts of the patients when they attempt to use humour as a tool to talk about or face a situation and (3) show a humorous practice towards the process or one's self.

This author shares the case of a patient who uses humour as a case for adaptation. It's the story of a woman whose marriage is about to end who asks for a first consultation. That same night, the therapist receives a call from the husband saying that his wife had taken an overdose of some medication and asked him what to do. Mindess quickly referred him to emergency services, who told him to give her a mixture of egg whites and salt. The therapist heard nothing more until the next day when the patient arrived for her appointment. She was very pale and told him about her anguish because her husband had been unfaithful in spite of loving each other very much, and in her despair she had taken an overdose of pills, hoping that her worried husband would call services. So she went to lie down waiting for the arrival of the rescue team. When she realised that her husband didn't know how to separate the whites from the yolks, she had to drag herself to the kitchen to show him how to make the prescription correctly to save her. As she was telling him her tragedy she began to laugh thinking how absurd the situation was. It was an act to break with the situation instead of remaining stuck with it, she laughed to overcome her pain. Thus she managed to synthesise the tragi-comic anecdote of her 15 years of marriage.

Mindess recommends even laughing at the practice itself and of the jokes made about psychotherapy, since nobody is free from making absurd or stupid errors; if one can leave the ideal space, perhaps the patient could be less rigid with himself.

Karyn Buxman also considers that for patients with mental disorders in psychyactric institutions and hospitals, as much for the patients as for the doctors treating them, humour offers important benefits, including the regeneration of the therapists (what P. Hawkins calls a resourcing, a necessary practice in coaching and its supervision). In this way, he provides advice for introducing humour in sessions, for doctors, nurses and/or carers of patients with mental disorders including those confined in mental institutions. In this advice, there are some outstanding recommendations.

1. Exchange anecdotes of ridiculous events. The patient and the caretaker can tell anecdotes about when they did something ridiculous: for example, when early one morning they left the house wearing odd shoes, the other can carry on by telling when he made a mistake with his socks, this encourages the telling of more stories. So this way an occurrence that seemed embarrassing at the time becomes funny and so leaves it in the past.

2. Remembering happy moments from childhood. The carers can help patients remember amusing or funny moments from their childhood, using the tools of visualisation. After a few silent breathing exercises, the patients can be asked to remember something that made them smile and then ask them – what can you see? Buxman warns not to do this with psychotic patients.

3. Play. Following the line set out in point 2, one can also invite the patient to remember a game or a toy. At first, it may be difficult but once started, the dynamics can be contagious for many patients it is interesting to join in.

4. Tell jokes, more jokes. Telling jokes needs practice. Practice on one's own seven times (nothing is less funny than a joke not well told, the narrator forgets what goes next, there is an interruption, etc.). The patients may not understand the whole joke, since their concrete or literal thinking may be dominating their psychic processes, but the group laughter is contagious and this allows them to feel socially accepted.

One should point out the inclusion of poetry in the form of the Limerick (The Limerick is a simple poem, made up of five lines, rhyming A A B B A, reminiscent of word games, so they can be fun). Here are two examples attributed to Edward Lear:

| There was a young lady from Niger | There was a young man from Peru |
|---|---|
| Who smiled as she rode on a tiger | Who found a dead mouse in his stew |
| They returned from the ride | Said the waiter "Don't shout! |
| With the lady inside | Or wave it about, |
| And the smile on the face of the tiger | Or the rest will be wanting one too" |

**Comic strips**

Each patient can bring his favourite and explain why he likes it and thinks it is funny. This, as well as creating an atmosphere favourable to humour, will allow them to share and strengthen social ties within the group.

**Play**

Can be non-competitive games or the idea of role playing, which also generate a transitional space (Winnicott) where the patient and the carer share the humorous space.

All the foregoing are humorous interventions that can be designed beforehand, different from those used in individual therapy where the therapist is waiting to see what the patient brings and the degree he has reached playing with words and fantasies, then to catch the opportunity for humour – the paradox, the joke – which can add beauty to the profound experience of "dancing to the rhythm of the session" with a patient.

## The therapy of laughter

In fact, although this contains an element produced by humour, we cannot consider this methodology within the humorous interventions as a production of the mind or of experience. This therapy – often consisting in exposing the group of patients to watch videos made specially to cause laughter and free corporal expressions such as a guffaw – has proved to give positive results in a feeling of well-being, although these are techniques to generate, mostly good humour, without playing with words or using incongruent situations and the patient's own experience.

One of the difficulties and challenges that this text has implied was the search in the bibliography for the effects of humorous interventions, what stands out most is precisely the ambiguity of defining humour. Martin and Ford (2018) shared the results of experiments and humorous interventions with mixed groups of patients. But these interventions refer mostly to the exposure of groups to different humorous videos and sitcoms vs control groups with documentaries or without videos and how this practice increases the feeling of well-being at the end of the study. Also, the study of the results obtained from hospital patients exposed to comedy programmes. Again, we are not dealing with humour as the capacity of victory and consolation towards oneself as proposed in the text, but rather the exposure to humorous material not related to the patient's specific situation, different from some therapists who can tell the patient a story or joke that is related to the conflict the patient has brought to the therapy session.

## Humour in the session of psychoanalysis

The patient asks the analyst why he answers his questions only with questions,
to which the analyst responds: Why not?
– Baker (1993, p. 959)

The study of humour during a session of analysis is intricate. The literature that has been written about it seems to be talking about many things at the same time. Therefore, it becomes such a vast field that it is necessary to limit it to be able to work with it. On one hand, the use of humour in sessions is criticised, but if we study the objections carefully we realise that we are not dealing with humour in Freud's sense (as established in Chapter 3), but more as a scorn.

What we may encounter during analytical work is: an initial joke without much wit. Then, the development of existing humour, or the development of humour when previously there was none, or mere moments of humour as the transference develops.

57

## Humour on the part of the patient

On the other hand, the matter gets more complex depending on who "invites" the humour during a session: the analyst or the patient himself. So for the moment, we shall revise what can be considered as coming from the patient, later what comes from the analyst and, finally, we shall look at possible contradictions of humour in session based on the ferocious article against humour in sessions by L. Kubie (1971, p. 127:7).

During analysis, moments of humour may arise. When this happens, it has the same characteristics as associations, which are also diversely determined, that is they have various levels and senses.

The point is that the moments in which humour arises should not be left without intervention, the same way as not leaving without an interpretation any formation of the unconscious which may arise during a session. As Baker points out, the impossibility of retelling a joke one has heard lies in the same mechanism responsible for forgetting dreams (Baker, 1993, p. 951).

## The joke as part of a session

What happens when a patient tells us a joke in a session? Should we laugh if we do not think it is funny? Should we be silent so as not to gratify the patient's attempt to seduce us? Should we interpret this attempt at seduction by the patient? In the first place, the telling of a joke by a patient should be received as one more element in the chain of associations, and therefore, as something that holds latent material. Zwerling (1955) underlined the existence of a favourite joke in some patients, which could offer many *insights* such as dream-like productions, early memories, etc. Although he accepts that it cannot be a technique, since some patients do not have favourite jokes, or even one. In fact, the emergence in the session of a recently told joke also holds a link to the conflicts the patient is undergoing. After analysing the jokes from several of his patients Zwerling found that:

> The joke served to manage anxiety by negation (including various patients); the subjects that caused most anxiety were those central to

the jokes, as if by laughing about something they could negate the emergence of anxiety.

(p. 112)

In this sense, Baker (1993) said that a joke manifests the sense of humour of the person telling it, but more important is it could be recognised by the analyst. The analytical understanding of jokes is indispensable, because without this, the patient's joke has little hope of being understood, just like someone telling a dream when the listener is someone who does not believe that dreams are important. The analysis of a patient's joke allows a glimpse of the sexual and hostile pulsations that are hidden in the joke, but just because it is a joke it is socially acceptable and allows for spontaneous pleasure (p. 951). In addition:

Baker provides an example of a patient of his whose telling of a joke which hid hostile desires: a 35 year old university student was married to a very dominant woman in front of whom he had a passive attitude. In a session one day he had the courage to tell a joke to the analyst and he begins: One day a couple is walking along the seashore when a pigeon flies over them and shits on the woman's new hat. She is annoyed and shouts at her husband not to stand there, to go and find a piece of paper, to which he replies "but the bird must be miles away by now!" The patient laughs a little embarrassed on the couch and the analyst says: "You are very envious". There was as intrigued silence for a few minutes. The patient asks "What? What do you mean? Envious? of whom?" the analyst replies "of the pigeon". This managed to do better work against his defences that were trying to hide the aggression, particularly against his wife, and his mother and maybe even to his therapist.

(p. 957)

Along these same lines, it is necessary to consider a certain complicity that takes place when one tells a joke. Whoever tells the joke as well as the patient that takes it up offers the content manifest in their histories. In this way, they also try to trap those who listen, as if to drag them into the experience of participating and reacting, to share their secret desires and to confirm the maliciousness of the derided yet feared authorities (Poland, 1990, p. 216).

It is also comparable with the patient who hopes to gain some gratification from the analyst, as well as the laughter expected as a result of the joke. However, in analysis, it is the frustration of that desire that allows a regression and a possible insight. This point is important to distinguish when the patient is trying to seduce through humour vs. when humour is the result of an insight or a "symptom" of progress.

Poland relates a humorous episode in analysis, where the revelation of joke elements of transference allowed to continue advancing in the analysis.

It was the case of a widow, she felt very isolated socially, through analytical work her ingenuity began to be acute and cutting, little by little it softened as the analysis advanced, and later new lines of analytical work were announced through jokes. When the transference became erotic, she told the joke about two elderly people in a nursing home. From her wheelchair, she says she can guess his age if he allows her to hold his penis in her hand. He accepts and after holding it for a few minutes she says he is 87. When he asks her how she had guessed, she replied that he had told her the week before. This humour allowed a bridge for the conflicts that had been displaced in the transference. Specifically, the entrance of the joke opened a space to access the sexual and aggressive motions that were in the transference. Her analysis made explicit what had formerly been implicit, as much with her brothers in her childhood, as with the transference, there were sentiments awakening in her, from her. The analyst says that this use of humour, above and beyond the content of any instance, revived a subtle attraction of the patient. The analysis of the sexual nature of the transference, revealed by the humour, expressed the fantasies and sadistic impulses, as well as the terror and despair that remained behind them. At the end of the analysis, this patient, who had begun the analytical process having a very limited social life, was already well known among her ever-widening circle of friends, thanks to her wit and acuteness. Even if she could be biting, she also understood that these acts could help her, as when this occurred she took it as a signal to review introspectively what might be happening to her (Poland, 1990, p. 208).

## Sketches of humour as a result of analytical work

There are some people who have a natural talent for wit that disappears due to the development of a neurosis or also a depression. Analytical work allows them to return to expressing the humour that existed originally.

It is possible that the analytical process, apart from being a way that frees oneself from the slavery of inhibitions and repetitions, is also a technique that generates new ways of looking at oneself, which results in new uses for humour, provided that the development of humour during analysis is never considered something to laugh about (p. 203).

Poland (1990) considered that to access humour (or what he calls mature humour) one should have already attained: the delay of the urgency of pulsations, the diminution of narcissistic demands, the respect for authenticity from others and the acceptance of a scale of reality greater than oneself. It means the possibility of accepting and recognising pain and loss without necessarily falling into hatred and despair.

In addition, the achievements that would show a good analysis of character would be: to tolerate uncertainty, ambiguity and the ability to integrate within oneself one's own vision of the world and the vast world of urgencies and contradictions, sentiments and ideas. Humour is the reflection of the analytical work carried out successfully.

Structurally, the presence of humour in the life of the patient is seen to be transformed and is a good indicator of the patient's state. It is an expression of an internal transformation in the subject.

Humour is an achievement in the development and a component in establishing relations with the object. It is, at the same time, a way of relating and also a technique for adapting (Giovacchini, 1993, p. 93).

For Giovacchini, the prognosis often depends on the patient's capacity to develop humour and to advance in a state of objective relation which is compatible with the formation of humour. With some patients, including some severe cases, there are occasional episodes, when in spite of their misery and suffering they can poke fun at themselves and, simultaneously, see and evaluate the horrible catastrophe of the outer world, but with a twist of irony. This type of humour is sometimes called black or gothic. For him, humour can also be a type of barometer that indicates the degree of integration of the ego, the same as other psychic processes that can show advances in the development or they can degrade regressively with the result of psychic disintegration (p. 94).

Next, we have the case of a patient who passed from a state of great rigidity to the possibility of observing herself humorously. For a long time, this patient had been very limited in her social relations so she considered herself to be an automat. This appeared in the transference and was worked in a hard and difficult manner, but from there on, the patient showed an enormous capacity for humour. Later on, during analysis, she even said things like this. "Okay, I'm going to look at reality, but as if I were a tourist!" (Poland, 1990, p. 204). It is fundamental to identify the difference between humour and a maniacal state, in which painful aspects are rejected and expelled, without being able to get hold of that painful content and diminish the aspects of persecution. The patient knows it is necessary to look at reality but she plays with it. She visits (as if asking herself: Now, what will I find?), instead of, in a manner of condemnation or persecution, going through a list of all the aspects of her reality.

There are also cases when, in the transference, patients begin to perform the comic role of their lives. This is a very important point to detect because it is here that the patient is using not humour, but rather comicity and laughter as a means to evade their pain or anger.

In this sense, Kris (1964) proposed that comicity is a mechanism of defence principally against anxiety, but the main incentive to play the role of comedian/clown is exhibitionism. One patient, he recounts, a young man, an exhibitionist, feeling shadowed by his brother, felt condemned to play the role of clown. When he found himself in heated discussions about political matters, he felt content by making an occasional joke. His ingenuity, resentment and aggression served him as defence against a passive oral fantasy, the desire to seduce through words. For a time, his role comic allowed him a certain balance, but it infringed distortions of his personality because of his desire to avoid competing with a stronger rival (p. 75).

# Defences and mocking laughter

The need to play the clown arises from an ambivalent, sadomasochistic character struggling against an intolerable burden of aggression, which causes an equally intolerable burden of guilt and punishment. The joke is an opportunity to disburden both the aggression and the guilt without resolving the hidden conflict and without maturing to a less ambivalent character (Poland, 1990, p. 219). In a patient with these characteristics, one should be very careful not to complete the voyeuristic circle that this type of patient tries to impose upon the analyst. In this case, when the patient arrives for a session, one can consider treating him as if he was a mental sadist, or as having a deep narcissistic pain regarding his brother. The humour would be counteracting his infantile narcissism, since it allows him to release the narcissistic images that he has about himself (personal communication by E. Ortiz).

Sometimes, during the analysis the attempts at humour misfire. For example, the following case: it is about a mature patient with a good sense of humour who suffered a great loss when his wife died in a car accident when he was driving. The patient experienced great pain; nevertheless, in a session clumsily attempting to find consolation he said: "it could have been worse, at least I had accident insurance" (Giovacchini, 1993, p. 84). The therapist was rather *shocked* by the crudeness of the comment, by this failed attempt to make the best out of a *bad* situation.

Regarding this case, Giovachini comments: The humorous attempt failed because the patient was overcome by his grief [...] the contained hostility that might have precipitated the accident rose to the surface, whereas the attempt to contain it by humour failed ... rather it would seem that the crude commentary hid the misery the patient was going through (p. 84).

It is also part of a maniac defence mechanism when the tone of humour is used in self-reproach. This is the case of a patient (Britton, 2003, pp. 135–136) who, during a session, started to comment – half laughing – about his fear of the dentist. Immediately following, he went on to comment on the horror he felt at books with explicit details of any pain being inflicted, and he accompanied this comment with an apparently casual laugh. This acute sensibility was a recurring theme in the analysis and the joking attitude of the patient created an atmosphere of superiority as if searching for an accomplice in the analyst to ridicule the fears of a frightened person in which he recognised himself. When the analyst suggested that he was trying to laugh off something that tormented him, the patient quickly responded with a state of discomfort and annoyance, taking up the fear of pain and the horrible fantasies of torture that he had been previously talking about in relation to his next visit to the dentist. In this case, the patient's self-mockery was an attempt (obviously failed) to divert his anxiety caused by a painful experience. C. Goetschy (2008) said that in this sense humour can be an obstacle for dependence in the therapy. One could think of a patient who uses humour to rid himself of the subject they were exploring in a session: his jokes being a way to avoid getting into contact with his feelings (p. 112).

Taking a defensive or a maniacal position is an attempt to avoid the oscillation between the positions of depression and persecution (Briton, 2003, p. 138). It is taking an omnipotent attitude in face of the world and its problems. This aimed at avoiding mental pain caused by anxiety and guilt, whether from a depressive or a paranoid schizophrenic position depending on the state of the patient's interior world at the moment of the "failed joke".

Baker considers that with borderline patients or with psychotic disorders one should not use humour, even if they have access to humour because of their character or personality. Given their constant inner feeling of being persecuted, humour is not on the same scale as with healthier characters. Or rather, they can tolerate it when it is about themselves, but not when the origin of the humour is external, especially from the analyst. In these situations that present masochistic or painful humour, the recommended interventions are interpretation or listening (Baker, 1993, p. 958). For example, we have an anecdote by Bleuer (1911) who had a patient who told him that according to Burgholzi there were four types of persons, patients, prisoners, those attending and those who were not in that place. Bleuer found this distinction humorous, however, he didn't laugh since the patient had not shown a sense of humour. A sense of humour in Winnicott's terms should be evidence of freedom, the opposite of the rigidity of defence that characterises the illness (p. 46)

In this sense, Giovacchini (1993) considered that humour or the lack of it are character traits that indicate how well adapted persons are to the external environment, as well as their progress in the therapeutic context.

There seems to be a direct correlation between the degree of psychopathology and a lack of humour. I believe that this generalisation, even with notable exceptions, shows as more valid the equation of the greater the pathology, the lesser the capacity to function effectively. Some seriously ill patients from a point of view of character can be very successful, at least financially (p. 95).

# About analytical interventions using humour

Another aspect would be that of the psychoanalyst's interventions that could be considered as bordering on humour. The fact that they keep a trait of "humour" does not mean they lose their analytical character. For Giovacchini, the analysts do not see their patients as tragic victims without hope. It is true that many patients have been treated in very cruel ways which have driven them to the depths of despair. Both the analysts and the therapists can feel the pain of their patients deeply, but in order to be effective clinicians, they need to remain in a position oscillating between not overburdening them with despair and a cautious optimism. This is a serious attitude, but not a sombre one and its purpose is to construct a transitional space in which humour can play an ever more important part (p. 107).

Greenson (1972) quoted the following contribution to Anna Freud's symposium "The widening Scope of Indications for Psychoanalysis" and indicates that there is a type of variant in technique determined by the personality of the patient and his transferences, as well as the reactions of the analyst towards them (p. 414). Therefore two analysts would never give exactly the same interpretation, it has been seen that there are no two patients who have been treated by the analyst in the same way. With some patients, we remain in absolute silence, with others, humour and even jokes can be part of a session. There are different ways in which we receive and say goodbye to patients and the degree to which we allow a real relationship with a patient to co-exist with any transference, fantasised. A. Freud, according to Greenson, considered that these unintentional variations in these responses are not imposed, not only because of the neurosis of the patients but because of the minor subtleties of their personalities, which may otherwise go unnoticed.

If we pay attention to these variations, the time it takes for our reactions and conduct to show and we cease to deal with them as unimportant-mere pleasantries, their observation and scrutiny will reveal important findings. In this way, we can observe the subtleties of the patient's healthy personality, the degree of maturity of the self, his capacity to sublimate, his intellectual talents and his ability to see his conflicts even if it is in a momentary and objective way.

Glover (1930) sets out in his article *The Vehicle of Interpretations* that during an analysis one tries to give interpretations in a tone free of stress, not very empathetic but neither lifeless, since this is the safest way to avoid the patient considering that the analyst is in counter-transference with him. However, this attempt may seem in vain since not even the most articulate tone of voice prevents the accentuation of some unconscious convictions. Here then is where we ask what form should these interpretations be given to the patient. We nearly get into the process of art, since it is a painful interpretation for the self, but articulated in such a way that it induces a discharge of an immediate *affect*, it even makes the patient laugh (assuming that he is capable of doing so) (p. 342). So we can consider that we are not talking about a type of regulation but rather an ability, of the possibility of doing so. The success depends most of all on the correspondence of the emotional mechanisms of the patient and the analyst. In other cases, it depends on how the analyst considers his capacity for ingenuity/wit and how he uses it without "affectedness". I consider this is how we can allow a possibility of using humour: avoiding the intention of making the analysis something humorous and all forms of sarcasm. Taken to the other extreme, Glover discusses how on occasions the use of scientific language allows some patients to unblock the difficulty of expressing verbal presentations which are highly charged with obscenities. Also, how in some cases "childish" words can cause greater problems than the directly obscene word. Thus one should gradually make the tech-nical material disappear from the "scene" (p. 342).

Yet, we can still say more in relation to what seems to be the par-ticular management of material that can be considered humorous. These interventions are not trying to be funny for the patient, as this would be a form of seduction. It is more like the return of something that the patient has brought. On occasions, it can be his own words, but it would have the effect of an invective (in the style of the cynics), a "demonstrative effect", which is patently obvious, but paradoxically could have the effect of a surprise. Reik says that a good interpretation always has the effect of causing surprise. So, the effect of humour could be considered as an interpretation of this type, which is a good interpretation. This is why to say that humour comes from the analyst is inexact, since the material really belongs to the patient, but passing through the analyst it can be returned in a humorous form. The analyst should place himself so that he can invert dialectically what the patient brings to him, and that in this exercise it can be made to cause humour (without being the objective of the task).

There are, however, certain moments when humour arises as an unexpected clarification of interior conflicts, moments not necessarily defensive, but rather which express new understanding and possibilities of integration (Poland, 1990, p. 2014). This is the case of a young Jewish lawyer, the son of a very controlling mother who threatened that if married she would commit suicide. At one point in his life, he meets a woman he falls in love with and wants to marry, but he says he cannot do so because the moment he tells his mother she threatens to kill herself using the gas oven. The subject emphasises his mother's suicide with anguish, to which the analyst responds gently: "I have the impression you will not free yourself from her so easily". After a long silence, he starts to talk about his relation with his mother which dates back to when he was a child and his hatred of her, of how he realises that she now needs him more than he needs her, and the implications in the transference, without it being necessary that the patient be tormented with oedipal interpretations and his death wish. After these interventions, the patients experienced surprise and then relief, of course from the psychic work. This is the typical pattern of what happens in a correct interpretation (Baker, 1993, pp. 957–958) (as suggested by Reik).

In addition, humour can be a vehicle to take a patient back to a transitional space of analysis when anxiety, terror, hatred or anguish had distanced him from it. A patient in a crisis of delirium complained to his analyst of how he was being conspired against by the Central Intelligence Agency to rob him of his ideas (the patient was a prominent scientist). He even had connections with the mafia (the analyst had an Italian name) they paid him $150,000 a year to pick his brains. The analyst responded that the mafia had no need to pay him anything since it was already included in the cost of the session, upon which the patient stressed how his analyst enjoyed extracting knowledge from him, he responded affirmatively and added that he found it fascinating and that he had learnt a lot from him.

At this point the patient's behaviour changed suddenly, the analyst says the difference was like night and day. The patient began to laugh when he understood that *to pick his brains* was just a metaphor with a benevolent sense. This then led to him telling how he had picked brains when he was a student and wanted to get inside the heads of well-known eminent scientists in order to know everything that they knew. His attitude changed completely, he went back to being playful and could review the *acting-out* sessions carried out the week before (Giovacchini, 1993, p. 102).

In this example, we can see how the second intervention of the analyst is mirroring in the sense that Winnicott suggests, and these words generated laughter at that moment as a way of bringing the patient back to the transitional space.

With this same patient who feared that his superior was going to rob him of his ideas, he said how was it possible that in the presence of such a brilliant and creative mind (with which he could identify), how could he blame his superior for wanting to know what he was working on (again he was being mirrored). This was said in a tone without sarcasm or irony, but in a good humour the patient laughed and playfully conceded the truth of the irony. While one uses the appropriate tone, the patient can come out of the darkness (return to the transitional space) without it being important if he was being told something enormously positive or confronting him directly with his irrational attitudes (Giovacchinni, 1993, p. 104).

In this particular case, Giovacchini says that he knew the intervention with humour could bring him back to the transitional space since the patient, in spite of his episodes and psychotic behaviour had never missed a session which showed that he was involved in the treatment. The laughter was spontaneously triggered by a deliberate intervention. However, he recognises that he felt sure so as to allow such spontaneity, particularly from his state of anger and darkness. Now if we look carefully at this example, in fact there is a humorous effect but the circuit drawn is simply how the analysts are repeating his same words except with a new meaning. And it is this new meaning that produces the surprise and later lets him discover what had him hooked in a state of anxiety (*pick his brains* in the sense of loss, or theft).

Another example of this type is that of a patient who is in transference with a lot of anger and hostility towards her analyst, who interprets this anger but she denies feeling so much hostility because she is scared of harming her object/analyst. The following day she says she has had a dream about a dirty baby *covered in shit*, to which the analyst says you are *covered in shit* and the patient immediately replies no, the analyst then says she is covered with happiness, at that moment the patient starts to laugh and finally says she thinks that yes, she is a little bit mad at her (personal communication by E. Ortiz).

Another insight that results in laughter, is the case of an adult patient who belonged to a very numerous, closely knitted family. Her family circle censured any form of therapy and she was always pressed to abandon her analysis. At the same time, she insisted on taking them to therapy (analysis) so that they could reflect on their own lives. She often spoke of feeling frustration and anger at not being able to change her family milieu or her environment. On one particular occasion, she pointed out how difficult it was for her to talk to her family when she was working to change things. At that moment, the analyst asked whether she was trying to change things for herself or for all the others. At this question, a memory came to her, and she said amid a sudden burst of laughter:

> I believe this reminds me of when I was a little girl and I would go up on the flat roof of our house. There I would spend hours trying to teach the turkeys that were kept there to vocalize, because I thought they were going to be able to speak.

At that moment, the force of her laughter made her realise all the vain efforts she had consistently made throughout her life, trying to change the world to her own liking.

Humour can subvert the relation between the subject and the other. Oscar Wilde once wrote "If this is the way Queen Victoria treats her prisoners, she doesn't deserve to have any" (Bergmann, 1999, p. 27).

This reminds us of an anecdote about Diogenes, after he was taken prisoner. Being about to be sold as a slave, they asked him what he could do, and he responded: "I know how to command men" (Laercio, 2006, p. 188).

Both these statements disrupt the relation between sovereign and prisoner: humour changes the positions of what one thinks one is. That is, it disrupts us, and puts us in doubt of what we think we are: it makes us face what is obviously happening to us although we are not aware of it.

On another occasion, a patient of mine who was terribly fixated with the idea of her husband meeting another women and she complained how this made her suffer greatly. This was one of the reasons for the consultation. She also mentioned her husband would go out with a male friend, whom she suspected of being a homosexual, and this anguished her because she considered him a bad influence on her husband. At that moment, I told her that if that was the case, he would like other men and there was nothing to be jealous about. Faced with this situation, she burst out laughing. At that instant, she understood that jealousy was her own constant way of relating, and it opened up the possibility of analysing what is a common undercurrent in cases of extreme jealousy, namely an unrecognised homosexual way to link to the image of the object which causes the obsession.

At this point, one can draw the analogy about what happens in a session. The analyst (the first person in the joke) makes a psychic effort to create an association of ideas or representations which can be absurd or incongruous, or he can use any other techniques for the creation and setup of jokes. He then tells the words to the patient, who receives them with great pleasure, allowing him to free that which had been repressed. Herein lies the surprise in the joke, as well as in the interpretation.

## Inspired interpretations within the theory of object relations

Meltzer (1978, p. 212) pushes what he calls "inspired interpretations". This means the analyst is exposed to the activities of the patient and, having an essentially personal experience, he can later use it with the help of his theoretical equipment, to explore the sense of the relation that is taking place in his consulting room. These interpretations are different from the routine ones in the following sense: when the analyst listens and observes the patient's behaviour, he assumes a pattern – or *gestalt* – in his mind, to which he later applies certain aspects of his "theoretical equipment" to explain things. Meltzer thinks that the abuse of technical terms in conversation with the patient is either a form of stupidity or an exhibition of megalomania. The *inspired interpretation* can be a statement without an explanation, requiring the analyst to abandon a pedagogical posture facing the infantile structures of the patient's personality, in favour of an attitude of camaraderie with the adult part of the patient, as in an adventure. Here, the interpretation is thought of as a metaphor open to various interpretations.

It is then evident at this point that we are considering a stage where the collaboration of the patient has reached a high level of confidence so that these moments of "instant camaraderie" can take place and the technique of shock can be put aside for a while. But if these occasions arise and the therapist only allows for a limited experience of sharing and camaraderie, there will be a reduction in the possibility of later sustaining the type of auto-analytical work after termination, which is necessary for further progress in the self-integration.

> I can feel within myself a clear and paradoxical call and a joke: analysts of the World dis-unite. You have nothing to lose but your self-idealization.
>
> (Meltzer, 1978, p. 224)

# Humour in the analysis of children

The analysis of children requires that interpretations be given in their own language, appropriate to their age. This includes children who are already in an age where latent narcissistic disorders can be present, where the abilities for interpreting reality and for judgement are at the service of maintaining a large ego.

Beren refers to sessions in which a little girl wants to play chess, but rejects established rules and invents new ones. One day her lady analyst says, "I have news for you, my uncle taught me to play chess but he did it all wrong". This results in a big smile on the little girl's face, and she asks how that was played. In this case, she managed to arrive at the intended meaning by way of an oblique approach. When the therapist made the child realise that someone was mistaken but not herself, she became interested in learning. The use of metonymy by the therapist, allowed for the continued flow of the therapeutic process (Sanville, 1993, p. 45).

Another instance is the case of an adolescent girl. Emma began her treatments at age 13, she suffered separation anxiety and went into long lapses of silence. In the third month of treatment, she broke the silence by laughing, saying she was thinking of a play she had written about a fairy godmother who turned into a witch, and a prince who was going to help but went to the pub and got drunk instead. She continued laughing and told the therapist that she was a fool. With following interventions of this type, the bouts of silence stopped and the girl developed a particular sense of humour. This surfaced first with her therapist and was later transferred to her parents, allowing for a certain capacity for ambivalence and ambiguity (p. 46).

Finally, a comment on the well-known case of *Richard*, referred by Melanie Klein. Richard, a ten-year-old boy, was treated by Klein for four months during World War II. He was incapable of establishing relations with other children of his age, his curiosity was severely inhibited, he was a hypochondriac and frequently fell into depression. The original text illustrates the psycho-analytical technique used by Klein in her work with children, as it records the improvement Richard shows throughout the process. Here, we will stress the fact that at the end of the treatment Klein points to the child's humour to show the improvement of his mental state. Specifically in sessions 76, 77 and 88, Klein (2003) detailed variations in Richard's mood in relation to the effect the different interventions had on the child. It is clear that this is about humour in a more general sense than those dealt with previously, but it certainly is a sign that the question of humour arises in a moment when the analysis is progressing, and defence mechanisms lose their rigidity.

# Humour in counter-transference

No doubt, the use of humour is also indispensable to analyse the counter-transference of the analyst. What are we referring to here?

Giovacchini underlines that for the analyst it is indispensable to maintain the same analytical attitude towards the counter-transference as towards the transference. This is to observe sentiments and events within a framework of tolerance and humour, including idiosyncrasies and limitations related to the personality of the therapist. Being rigid and judgemental in the counter-transference is as negative as attitude as it would be in one's conduct towards a patient.

But being prejudiced also requires a sense of humour (Meltzer). Human weaknesses are not an object of mockery, nor of condemnation of the super-ego, nor a motive for humiliation by the id. If the analyst does not condemn these weaknesses in his patient, why should he do so against himself? Humour allows the analyst to look at himself as an object of interest, of study, which allows him not to take himself very seriously. Recognising the attitude and conduct of the analyst allows for a sensation of freedom that lets him take a dramatic event and play with its metaphors (p. 107).

Meltzer has worked and written bravely and honestly in relation to counter-transference. He stresses the need to investigate the intrusion of the un-analysed psychopathology of the analyst as another factor for understanding the phenomenon of the consulting room. Nevertheless, this is indeed a problematic and delicate subject because it becomes discretely and comfortably entrenched in theoretical formulations, so when the open discussion happens, passions often flare and become emotional debates, as irrational as the ones we expect to see when talking about politics and society (p. 210). If counter-transference in the analysis could be looked at through the lens of humour, much more could be learned from it. The discussions about what happens in an analytical session would be more open and the debates confronting different schools and groups of psychologists would be less contentious.

# Humour. An analysis of fears and realities

Traditionally, the terms joke, humour and comical have been closely associated and seen as something spontaneous. In fact, they are all different: they are variously related to unconscious, repressed contents of a sexual nature, and therefore mainly linked to sadistic intentions, which set a sort of invisible line that "bans" the use of truly spontaneous, fresh or humorous expressions.

H. Doolittle (1956, p. 116) recalled an occasion when she asked the analyst Walter Schmideberg when and how he got the idea that led him to relate certain cases of neurotic states of megalomania and omnipotence with childhood and youthful fantasies. The latter conventionally replied that Freud did not *"come up with"* ideas. Doolittle wondered if this was really true, but Schmideberg repeated what was obvious: that all the corpus of work was founded on precise, scientific and accumulated observations. This response did not correspond to the question: she wanted to know the exact moment of that flash of inspiration when something went "click". What had sounded, what had shouted in the mind of Freud? This passage seems to reflect the rigidity in the posture of the first analysts, in the way that discoveries were not seen as an occurrence/idea of one day, but as the result of a long, cumulative process. This is true of course, and the question posed by a free spirit might not have an answer, since it is impossible to think of the moment of the "spark". And yet, it is also true that the discovery must have started from a particular *insight*.

So, the appearance of any of these phenomena in a session, for some analysts, has come to be seen as a dangerous weapon of sorts.

We coincide with Bader in that the expressions of humour by the analyst can have multiple meanings for the patient. On the one hand, they can reinforce resistance as much as they project painful emotions for; but they can help deepen the analysis and aid in the healthy growth of the patient.

Next, we shall delve into the text of Lawrence Kubie, who has a distinct posture regarding humour: in general terms, he holds that it should be proscribed from sessions. An analysis of his text helps to distinguish what happens in each of the cases he presents, and whether he is really talking about humour.

Lawrence Kubie (1972) was a famous psychiatrist/psychoanalyst, the orthodox leader of the "New York analysts". While he was in charge of the teaching clinic at the University of Maryland he published his radical posture against the use of humour in therapeutic work, called *The Destructive Potential of Humour in Psychotherapy*. It should be noted that in the text, the terms *therapist* and *analyst* are used indistinctly, as if the position of one or the other had no variants during the encounter with the analytical patient and the therapeutic patient, in spite of it being necessary to recognise how both hold a privileged place for the patient. This text is one of the most debated in the bibliography related to humour, and it is a required reference in the study of the use of humour during therapy.

Kubie maintains that *humour has a highly destructive potential, that it is a dangerous weapon*, and that *the mere fact that it amuses and entertains the therapist and gives him a pleasant feeling is no evidence that it is a valuable experience for the patient or that it exerts any changes in the patient towards a way to health.*

In the particular case of psychoanalysis, humour is never done for the satisfaction of the analyst; therefore the sensation of well-being mentioned by Kubie describes the function of a *biased joke* rather than that of humour. The biased joke can be hostile or obscene and is aimed at aggression, satire or defence. Even the *intellectual joke* does not have a connection with any of these tendencies, since he recognises that some jokes have the motive of a *conceited impulse to show off our own wit by giving a show*, and that *this is an instinctual equivalent to sexual exhibitionism.* These types of motivation are definitely to be avoided, particularly when we use humour in analytical work with patients, where we should stress that it is definitely not considered humour.

Kubie considers that one can "bribe" a patient into accepting humour, and the patient can feel obliged to accept it (p. 38). However, it is important to clarify that given the way Kubie expresses himself, he is referring to a biased joke that would not have the subtleties nor the elegance – let alone the therapeutic effects – of true humour.

It is important to check when the analyst's own humour can be beneficial or become a danger. Given that discourse is a particularly strong form of action in an analytical situation, humorous discourse is charged with very potent emotions (Poland, 1990, p. 220). It is obvious that if humour is used to express aspects of the analyst's own conflicts, the patient will not develop insights and his progress will very probably be inhibited. For Meltzer, this vulnerability of the analyst lies in the incomplete state of our methodology, which is vague about the formulation of our techniques. There is a wide gap between what analysis can describe, what we think happens and what really happens.

In this way, we recognise that our view of what is "funny" can be a double-edged sword. Humour that debases or deprecates the analyst runs the risk of missing the negative transference of the patient. Kubie (1972) advises never to use humour in a session of analysis. But once again, this instance is not considered humour either.

Analysis is the patient's show, not the analyst's. Analysis is not a group therapy of two. The humour of the analyst contributes best if used sparingly. Analysis is not supposed to be a humorous experience.

Kubie says the therapist should always remember that he is unlikely to be the first one to find something funny in the life of the patient – in his ideas, his behaviour or in his symptoms – and that the patient certainly does not have much to laugh about (p. 39). It should be more than evident: someone who smiles or laughs when he views painful material either has a sadistic tendency, or at least has a fear of being sarcastic as a defense mechanism. Finally, Kubie says that mockery towards the patient on the part of the analyst is in fact disguised hostility, caused by untreated childhood conflicts. Such attitude is not only unprofessional: it reinforces the patient's perception of the pattern of mockery he has experienced throughout his life. Moreover, this failure is amplified by the fact that the analyst holds a privileged place as "the love object" of the patient, by means of transference, and mockery is also thus amplified in the patient's view.

Kubie also refers to a case study of a patient who had left two previous therapists because they dealt lightly with her and joked about her symptoms and fantasies, an attitude that caused her great pain (p. 39).

In this sense, we should consider that both therapists were not using humour but rather trying to avoid the mental pain of the patient, without assimilating "the alpha particles" in the sense described by Bion and, terrified at the idea that the patient's chaos would invade them, they avoided confronting her grief. Kubie tells of another danger of humour: it blocks the analyst's "incognito mode" which protects the patient from the therapist. He even declares that in his years as a supervisor he has not found a single case where humour has been beneficial to the patient (p. 41).

Nevertheless, at the end of his article Kubie marks an important difference – probably not realising that this could give new meaning to his article – as he distinguishes the critical disparity between laughing with someone and laughing at someone. He finally accepts that as the patient gradually gains self-knowledge, an increased understanding of humour can sometimes help him use new insights to limit, control or even guide the symptomatic expressions still present in his neurosis. It seems that he is not so far away from the premises put forward in this work after all.

In fact, the position of humour is consistent with the rule of abstinence. It would be dangerous if the use of humour were to prevent problematic emotions and fantasies from surfacing, but rather used to impose the "psychology" of the analyst.

Meltzer says: *I think—as I think about all psychoanalysis— that if it is not enjoyable it is not good; I like to enjoy it. The use of humour and mischief seems very important, not only in supervision, but also in analysis. I like all sessions to end with a smile.* For Meltzer, the attitude towards humour – like the attitude towards many other things – changes towards the end of the analysis (Berman de Oelsner and R. Oelsner, 1999, p. 13).

# Humour in coaching and coaching supervision

## A space to play and to use humour

In this section, we shall consider the direct use of humour in the field of coaching and coaching supervision. More specifically, we will see it as a space for formative and normative reflection because humour can appear in any human activity. In the first part of this book, we talked about the history of man, and then about the metapsychology of humour and its use in sessions of psychotherapy. We will now focus on the direct, pragmatic use of humour during the process of coaching and coaching supervision, so it will be necessary to move from the theoretical to a more practical approach. This section is thus meant to provide ideas and tools to use humour positively and ways to avoid its potential pitfalls.

We will explore what are the functions of humour and how it can be used specifically in the fields of coaching and coaching supervision. In essence, the same tools can be used in both practices, but due to their distinct nature, special elements need to be highlighted for each of them. We will first look an overview of each one, showing the common elements of both, and going into more detail where appropriate.

## The basics of coaching

Coaching is a relatively new profession that continues to grow steadily. The number of ICF coaches was 41,000 in 2020 compared to 2,000 coaches in 1999. The total estimated coaches in the world are 71,000 in 2020 as per the 2020 ICF Global Coaching Study. It is a practice that takes research and

DOI: 10.4324/9781003154310-6

studies from other fields, but it has its own spirit and merits. The European and Mentoring Coaching Council (EMCC) and International Coaching Federation (ICF) are associations that seek to ensure the standards and quality of coaching. As per Hawkins and Turner, "coaching is a relational dialogic practice in which at least two individuals join to discover new meaning and co-create new thinking and ways of being and doing in the world between them". By doing these, the individual can achieve goals and transformations through a conversational process.

# The use of humour in coaching

Until now, there is little bibliography related to humour in coaching and it is almost non-existent in coaching supervision. The use of humour in coaching is a subtle practice, which has not been openly dealt with, due to the difficulty implicit in trying to describe it. Problems arise because its use is unique to each occasion, but also because it can come in so many different forms in a session that the collection and classification of cases would be a daunting task. Jem Gash (2017) summarises this well in his book *Coaching Creativity* and acknowledges that "in coaching, we use humour in many ways: through our questions, during reflecting back to our clients, to shift pace or mood and perhaps when a challenge is needed". We also use it to build relationships and perhaps to play down our opinions or "self-efface" when required. Shifting "states" can help take our clients into an expansive, open, disruptive place, full of rich learning. Simple questions like these need to be used with caution, but can be very effective" (p. 167):

- How are you taking this all too seriously?
- In what way could you laugh at this situation?
- How do you find yourself ridiculous?
- What might you look back upon, in the future and really laugh at?

However, using these questions requires the coach to take a risk, but letting go of certainties and taking risks can be hazardous propositions! As Gash makes clear, this requires a robust working relation that lets the coach venture into these questions. We will offer more specific tools that can be used for coaches to introduce humour in the session.

# Coaching supervision, a space for reflection

It is necessary to briefly restate what Supervision in Coaching is, as it is a relatively recent practice whose formal training began in the second decade of 2000. Supervision in Coaching is a space for reflection in which the supervised subject "visits" his Coaching practice. It is a learning opportunity, and therefore an occasion for growth. As mentioned by D. Goldvarg (2017), in a session of supervision both participants (supervisor and supervisee) distance themselves from the issue at hand "to see what is happening from a different point of view" (p. 32). This new space creates the possibility to see complex situations and multiple solutions. The topics can begin with one's own subjectivity and point towards profound questions about the ethics of how coaching is practised.

The European Mentoring and Coaching Council defines supervision as

> the interaction that occurs when a mentor or coach brings their coaching or mentoring work experiences to a supervisor in order to be supported and to engage in reflective dialogue and collaborative learning for the development and benefit of the mentor or coach, their clients and their organisations.

The functions of supervision include:

- Developing the competence and capability of the coach/mentor.
- Providing a supportive space for the coach/mentor to process the experiences they have had when working with clients.
- Encouraging professional practice related to quality, standards and ethics.

To note, within the supportive/reflective space ethical dilemmas are very important in supervision of coaching since "sooner or later the Coach will find himself facing situations where he can feel divided as to different paths to follow. For example, when a client recommends his boss or a relative... the dilemma is whether to work with the person recommended, or if working with that person might have negative consequences on his client's process"(Goldvarg, 2017, p. 33). This is not necessarily so, but it is necessary to ask the question. It is part of the ethical basis in which the coach must be constantly questioning himself.

Supervision in Coaching has unique dialectics because the supervisee and the supervisor share a learning process. It is different from a mentorship where one party is the expert and the other receives the advice: the space for reflection allows for symmetry in the learning process, even though the supervisor is in charge of directing it.

In the existing bibliography about Supervision in Coaching, it is easier to find what supervision does than what it is about, because the most important thing about Supervision in Coaching is the result reached by the experience. Among these possibilities, E. Turner and Palmer (2019), in *The Heart of Coaching Supervision,* mention that it:

1. *Provides fresh perspectives.*
2. *Attends to the quality of what we (Supervisors) do and ensures safe practice.*
3. *Attends to how we (Supervisors) develop ourselves personally and professionally.*
4. *Requires us (Supervisors) to grow higher levels of self-awareness and to work on ourselves, as we are "the tool".*
5. *Enables resourcing of the coach, mentor, leader and supervisor.*
6. *It allows for interconnecting many stakeholders.*

(pp. 2–3)

Peter Hawkins and Shohet (2012, p. 5) also proposed a way of thinking for supervision, which he describes as

> a joint endeavour in which a practitioner with the help of a supervisor, attend to their clients, themselves as part of their client-practitioner relationships and the wider systemic context, and by so doing improve the quality of their work, transform their client relationships, continuously develop themselves, their practice and the wider profession.

Supervision is an innovative practice, not only because it is rather new but because it includes new thinking about the systems we form part of, not only about the individual work of the supervisee. For many years, both in therapy and coaching, the work was directed exclusively towards the person who resorts to this practice. The Supervision in Coaching is a conscious and rigorous effort to integrate reflection into the dynamics and needs of a broader system.

It is all so recent that this text is merely an observation of what is going on right now in the supervision practice. It continues to evolve as we talk about it. This is why it is a crucial moment to reflect about leveraging humour as a tool since its appearance is in the order of extraordinary incidence of time, content and insight.

When this topic was presented for the first time at the Americas Coaching Supervision Conference, attendees were asked: What were your negative thoughts or concerns about a conference on Humour in Supervision? Among the "negative thoughts" arose the fear that it might seem a lack of respect towards the "supervised subject" or that it might be construed as mockery or a lack of seriousness in the conversation. In general people a afraid of opening up about delicate matters and react either negatively or fearfully to the reaction of the other person, in this case, the supervisor. An extremely sensitive person might experience the use of humour as a validation of his fears that there is something about himself or his practice deserving of mockery.

These fears are justified, as was mentioned in previous chapters about the different forms of comicality and how humour is a small, privileged fraction of the forms of what is comical. In the following paragraphs, we will examine the need for introducing the tools of play and humour in order to privilege a safe space in which the supervision relationship can flourish.

# Functions of humour

It is in our interest to understand that humour can have two basic main effects in coaching and coaching supervision: psychological and as a way of learning. I also propose a third effect and is its capacity to generate a way for new thinking.

## *Psychological functions*

There are three known psychological functions of humour (Martin and Ford, 2018).

We should mention that a joke, metaphor or story could have one of these functions (social, communication and psychological):

1. Humour has positive effects on cognitive and social processes. Social functions, such as mediation. This is a manner of sharing social norms, establishing social links and finding common ground. Humour reveals that we are all human beings struggling to live and make a good sense out of it.

2. Humour communicates both positive and negative messages and can be used as a tool for insight and deliver training to discuss management, to shift topics and to enable people to see things from different perspectives. This is a delicate task of transmitting an idea that opens a space for reflection. It is probably the aspect that has the greatest impact on the formative part of Supervision of coaching. The other two aspects would be for establishing a link with the supervisor and in the space for generating confidence and relief so as to be able to have bolder conversations.

3. Humour as an emotional leveller. For example, it relieves tension so that one can overcome adversity (as in Chapter 2, where Freud reveals how humour, jokes and comicality share the same liberating characteristics). Humour helps oneself to take things easy, to keep plunging ahead, to release stress and tensions and create mirth: we all experience anger, and humour helps to take things easier and continue with life. It can also help to reduce fear. Such is the case in the story of *The Ghost of Canterville:* there is a terrifying ghost who has caused madness and the death of several people who visited the castle. However, the nonchalance with which Mrs. Otis speaks to him makes the ghost's structure of fear disappear. It is the same as what is described in the beginning of the book *The Name of the Rose*: the fear of laughter leads to losing the fear of God, from the Abbot's point of view. This emotional function makes it an indispensable tool in the supervision of coaching. If we consider that supervision is a space for reflection, as well as for encounter and discovery, humour can help reduce tensions or sudden outbursts of emotion.

It is for these reasons that the study of humour and its pragmatic use cannot be disregarded. Numerous examples for humour as a way of coping will be provided at the end of this chapter.

## *Humour is a way of learning*

As we saw in Chapter 1, humour has been a form of learning since the time of the Greeks, because it can challenge reality to provide new perspectives, in exactly the way Diogenes did (Part I).

There is evidence (Parkin, 2010) on how humour has proved to be a powerful partner in the learning process. In a study conducted in 1988 at Indiana University, researchers found that learners exposed to humour were more receptive to information and developed a better rapport with their teacher. They also found that when students were given key learning points, followed by a humorous story, they remembered the key points much better than when there was no story (p. 18).

## *Humour as a way to divergent thinking*

There is a very important effect of humour based on its mechanisms. Whether we consider it as a paradoxical mechanism (Cognitive) or as a way of expressing double meaning (Psychoanalysis), humour makes it possible to see two different things at the same time, through plays on words. This trait enables us to put additional meaning on a known concept or idea and by doing this, humour introduces the possibility of divergent thinking, which in turn widens our scope to a new range of possibilities: exactly the same effect sought by good questioning. Thus it is a way to break free from the attachment to single interpretations, to be able to free oneself from fixed ideas and force new connections to be made. This is the way of the Sufis as stated by Abu-Said, son of Abi-Khair: "To be a Sufi is to detach from fixed ideas and from preconceptions, and not to try to avoid what is your lot".

When we hear a good joke or humorous idea, there is a fraction of a second in which the mind is registering the first, literal sense of the idea as the second interpretation is "coming in". That moment is fascinating because we can see the mind at work, bringing together new connotations to a base idea. The term is currently used in the generation of creative processes. Interestingly, humour is at the root of the possibility of bringing new meanings and ideas to life. Humour and creativity are character traits that are commonly paired.

# Coping with COVID-19 examples

There is plenty of positive use for humour as a tool in stressful or painful situations. The space in supervision is a space for growth that includes introspection, which in many cases is not easy and it does require effort to overcome uncertainty or anxiety. In this sense, humour allows for hope, to be able to get through difficult situations.

Specifically, humour can be used to get through painful moments. Ritz writes in *The Humour of the Survivor* (Salameh and Fry, 2004) that when people are facing disaster, humour is often a strategy to get through catastrophic moments, something like a survival mechanism at moments requiring great resilience. In this sense, supervision is an exercise in resilience, understood as the ability of people to feel better quickly after something unpleasant has taken place. In fact, the speed of recuperation is not the most important thing, but rather the recovery after a mishap or something painful. The presence of humour indicates that the subject has been dealt with and one can move on. This is not done by negation but by unqualified acceptance. Humour can be seen as an aid to get through difficult moments. It can arise naturally from the supervisee himself, as a small victory, such as being able to see a funny side of the situation; or it can also come from a warm gesture from the supervisor. So, within supervision we can find the same wit and humour as with people who are experiencing catastrophe: again, humour is specific to situations.

Next, I shall show various humorous occurrences that have arisen over the period of the COVID-19 pandemic in 2020. The pandemic has yielded a transcultural phenomenon because most of the world experienced a similar situation. We have gone beyond the limits of the imagination in a way that has become common to all. During the early stages of shutdown, there were moments that caused anxiety, anger, disbelief… sensations of finding oneself in an absurd and unreal situation. These are profoundly emotional moments that are now common to millions of people.

We saw an outpour of humorous elaborations about these phenomena on the Web. One brilliant example is the Twitter account @SoVeryBritish. It is unusual to see Twitter quotes in an academic text,

85

but in a globalised world it is the web that provides the most material, and in the case of the use of humour during shutdowns it was almost immediate. In addition, the humour produced in the pandemic meets the definition of "transcultural". By contrast, we can see the nature of jokes about football or baseball teams: they cannot be transcultural since they need the particular history of the team or its local cultural setting. Following are some examples of tweets in which humour works based on the four functions that Ritz proposes in his book:

1. Humour is a way of managing anxiety when a situation cannot be changed. This is a profound recognition of a situation with no possibility of change, but one can play at controlling it through simple ingenuity.
   Examples
   VeryBritishProblems (@SoVeryBritish).
   "Recreate being in nightclub:
   1. Sit nervously in the corner of your living room
   2. Occasionally shout "WHAT?"
   3. Wonder how you ended up here
   4. Vow never to do this again
   5. Lose your jacket". 19/04/20. 10:44. Tweet.

   VeryBritishProblems (@SoVeryBritish).
   "How to pretend you're in a gym
   1. Place small towel over shoulder
   2. Wonder around the room while texting". 30/04/20. 21:06. Tweet.

2. Humour as a way to express annoyance. Annoyance is a difficult emotion to express. In his writings on *Pediatrics and Psychoanalysis,* Winnicott says that the problem of the world is not so much aggression as the fear of it. It is true that controlling aggression maintains social ties and part of adapting to reality consists in making sure one's own emotions leave the surface intact. So that showing one's annoyance through sarcasm, in an interior conversation, can liberate the exasperation without harming a relationship.

Examples:

VeryBritishProblems (@SoVeryBritish). "Wondering if the jogger striding towards you is expecting to pass through your body or for you to simply disappear into thin air". 03/15/20. 12:15. Tweet.

VeryBritishProblems (@SoVeryBritish). "Feeling certain you give off a "don't worry, I'm definitely the one who crosses the road" vibe each time someone stroll confidently along the pavement towards you". 23/04/20.9:26. Tweet.

3.  Humour as a way of finding common patterns of behaviour and at the same time reinforcing the cohesion of the group or community. On difficult occasions of isolation, it is very easy to feel that one has lost the sense of belonging to a community. In cases of pain or sadness, one experiences a sort of isolation from the place where everyone else is. Here it is important to remember, practically as a caricature-like trait as we saw in Chapter 2, how we can find ourselves as human beings going through the same tasks in spite of the difficulties and geographical locations.
    Example:
    VeryBritishProblems (@SoVeryBritish).
    "Video call background" personalities:

    *"I am very Smart"*
    *-Lots of unread books*
    *"Stay out of my private life"*
    *-A blank off-white Wall*
    *"Wild Child"*
    *-Garden*
    *"Harry Potter"*
    *-A small cupboard*
    *"Wine drinker"*
    *-Kitchen worktop*
    *"I have kids"*
    *Closed echoing bathroom, 20/04/20. 12:46. Tweet.*

Now working from home might have become an entrenched habit. But when it all came as a shock all the productive force was trying to surmount the crisis by replicating meetings and formality just as it would be prior to the confinement, when "business as usual" tried to compete for space and silence in households not prepared for remote work. By looking candidly at these jokes, we see how humour reveals our own distress and misfortunes but it also embraces us.

4. Humour offers rationalisation as an alternative to accept a disaster. In fact, there never are any explanations, but from an absurd position, so absurd as to be inexplicable, comes the possibility of acting as if we understood what happened. For example, that time plays a very relative time, that doesn't seem to move on in spite of what the calendar and our common sense tell us.

Examples:

VeryBritishProblems (@SoVeryBritish). "After nearly three months, today is the last day of May". 31/05/20. 9:17. Tweet.

VeryBritishProblems (@SoVeryBritish). "Not going out is much more fun when it is possible to go out". 29/05/20. 21:09. Tweet.

These four ways can be found at any moment in coaching supervision in a playful manner to avoid falling into tragedy, a way out of anger, finding consolation in being part of a community or teasing the absurd. They can be identified in session as ways of how the coach faces the overwhelming events in life. In any case, we can see humour as a possibility of hope, which helps us to digest and carry on with strenuous situations.

In all previous cases, we can see how humour is a part of the self, looking after the other part of the self. It works by telling us that it somehow understands the situation is very difficult, but that it can be seen in another way, and that perhaps we may feel better if we can laugh at it.

# 6 | Tools and pragmatic use of humour

## What does it take to create humour?

Having learnt about humour and found it desirable, this is a most natural question. Besides specific vehicles for it that will be shared shortly, there are certain traits that make humour natural and spontaneous. There are several of them, but I think they can be summarised in the following graph (Figure 6.1).

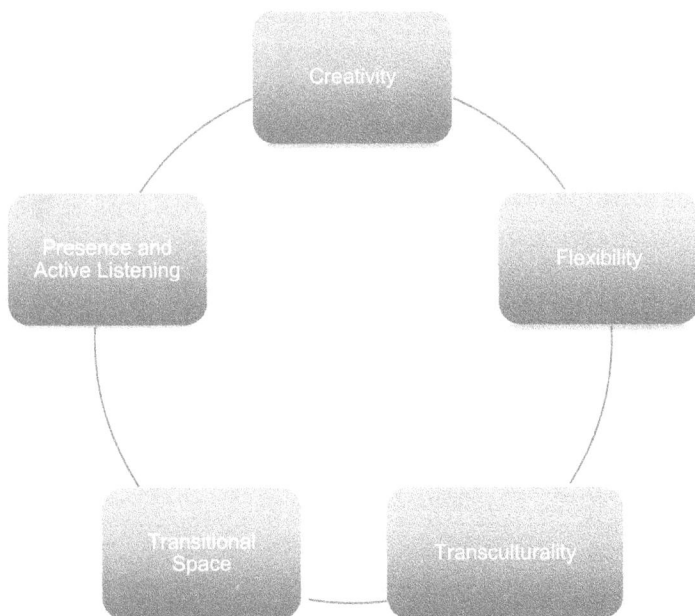

*Figure 6.1* Circuit of 5 elements that are needed to create humour.

DOI: 10.4324/9781003154310-7

# Creativity

This is the capacity to transform, give birth or materialise an idea, a work of art or a new way of doing things. It is a highly desirable human activity, but it does not always come naturally. There have been lengthy discussions about whether it is an innate ability or whether it can be developed through certain practices and/or favourable environments.

Children tend to be more creative than adults. But as we grow up, through the natural acceptance of roles and mindframes in the path of education, creative capabilities diminish dramatically.

Culture and its manifestations are the core resources for creation. Being able to learn about the world, experiencing other ways of life, understanding diverse expressions for emotions such as love and passion, becoming familiar with a variety of disciplines and hobbies, landscapes and foods, philosophies and music: these are raw materials that enlarge the inner world and have a floating "unconscious knowledge", as Lacan would say, that will allow for new connections to form, thus allowing for new results.

Creativity requires new associations of ideas. In language, words are the units through which we construct these associations. There is a beautiful scene in the movie *Il Postino* by Michael Redford, in which the poet Pablo Neruda explains to his postman what a metaphor is, but it is the postman that ends up with the best insight. Here is the dialogue:

- I felt seasick while hearing your poem.
- Because...
- I can't explain it. I felt like...like a boat tossing around on those words.
- Like a boat tossing around on my words? Do you know what you've done, Mario?
- No, what?
- You've invented a metaphor.
- Really?
- Yes, you have!
- But it doesn't count because I didn't mean to.
- Meaning to is not important. Images arise spontaneously.

*- You mean then that…for example, I don't know if you follow me…*
  *that the whole world…the whole world, with the sea, the sky…*
  *with the rain, the clouds--*
*- Now you can say "etcetera".*
*- Etcetera! So… the whole world is a metaphor for something else?*
  *… I'm talking crap.*
*- No, not at all.*

*The whole world is a metaphor for something else.* Every image, every word has the potential to create or evoke something else. Words provide us with an infinite resource for representing an image with another image, hence the more words we have, the greater the potential for creativity. The world is very rich for those who learn to see it. Creativity, in a way, is also the result of being able to experience the richness of the world.

# Flexibility

This is a key attribute of humour and also an indispensable ability for facing our current, fast-paced times. It is the capability to adapt to the environment, to anticipate change and even to yearn for it.

Flexibility requires being agile in jumping from a topic, to a place, to an emotion… to go around the world of ideas and come back if needed within a few seconds.

It is also about being open to new thoughts, processes and ideas. For example, classical Athens welcomed foreigners to become a part of their daily life. These *metics,* as they named them, were architects, philosophers or tutors for wealthy families. They had both rights and responsibilities and through both knowledge and active participation in society, they greatly contributed to the flourishing of Athens.

*Diversity* is a key element to both creativity and flexibility. By learning from new cultures and their ways of thinking, we widen our own scope of mental possibilities.

Flexibility is also a way of life. When faced with a new situation, it lets you react to it despite never having experienced it before. This might seem trivial, but there is a very large amount of people that tend to be very rigid towards new situations and want to react in ways that are already familiar to them, even if the situation itself is unfamiliar. Much of the power of coaching and the magic effect of coaching supervision relies on being able to provide flexibility, "loosening up" ideas that are entrenched in the mind of the client. These entrenched ideas are commonly called "limiting beliefs". By asking precise questions, we allow the mind of the client to wander to different new places: places he could not have reached without the dialogue. This process makes the limits begin to "soften", and thus the thinking space grows wider.

We are born with a very flexible mind: children have an incredible capacity to constantly adapt to their environment. The mind is thus very elastic by nature, but as the process of adaptation and growing up continues, it starts to lose this nimble quality, as a fixed environment makes it attach to it in an equally fixed way. Knowing the rules provides comfort and eventually, it creates resistance to continue experimenting. Changes in our lives, though difficult, make us flexible: as when a child goes to a new school, or when moving into a new city or country. But not every change needs to be this dramatic: modifications in our daily routine, trying new exercises, meeting new people and launching new projects are also events that keep us flexible.

Travel is an exercise in flexibility. Being able to wake up in a different place, eating unfamiliar food at schedules different from our own, greeting others in new, exotic ways: these are all activities that require an effort, however, small. It is very common to hear people say that they are used (attached!) to their own pillows or mattresses, or to the way the sunrise illuminates the room early or late. This is a sign of being too adapted/attached to our own spaces, and maybe introducing a little novelty or even "discomfort" to our lives through these changes, to keep us on our toes, is not a bad thing after all.

Flexibility is also in music and language, hence its importance for humour. Being able to trespass limits and meanings is a key trait that provides movement and allows for new connections to happen. Humour is also about connecting things and ideas that originally seemed completely unrelated in our set, logical patterns.

# Transculturality

We've gone through travel, culture and words, so it is only natural we should turn our attention to transculturality.

Humour requires us to be specific: that we should pay attention to the timing and the context of our words. As an example, let us first see the title of one of Oscar Wilde's plays: *The Importance of Being Earnest,* an excellent example of humour being nearly untranslatable. Wilde's text was first translated into Spanish as *"La importancia de llamarse Ernesto"*, simply using the Spanish equivalent of the name Ernest. In fact – for in Spanish there is no importance whatever in being called "Ernesto" – the character could might as well have been named Juan or Guillermo. Here lies the impossibility of making the name in Spanish the vehicle to carry the much more profound meaning that the original word game does. It is not necessary to explain that the word *earnest* is defined as being serious and determined, especially too serious and unable to find one's own actions funny. Therefore the play on words with the name *Ernest* and the word *earnest* does not hold in this translation. In the play, witty humour makes the principal character the exact opposite of an earnest person, so humour re-frames rigidity and allows one to think of situations from another point of view.

Although the play is very entertaining in any language, it is clear that we have missed the humorous pun of the title in that translation. A much better option was later given by Alfonso Reyes, one of Mexico's greatest writers. His translation was *La Importancia de Ser Severo*, a wonderful construction using the proper name Severo, which also means *severe* or *solemn*, and the fact that the verb *Ser* ("to be") can be indistinctly used to indicate "being" or "being named". It thus takes great talent and reflection to be able to translate humour properly.

We can see that not only does language offer a sizeable difficulty for attaining the universality of a joke, but so do culture and context. So what is translatable? What can be applicable in different environments? And especially, what can be done in such a global practice, as coaching and coaching supervision?

In this sense, it is necessary to define and differentiate the terms *Intercultural, Multi-cultural* and *Transcultural*. Here, the first question arises: What is transcultural humour, particularly in the area of coaching? Let us first establish these definitions:

- Multicultural includes people of different races, religions, languages and traditions. In this case, we may think of the example of a city with different ethnic groups, all having rights and services according to their cultures and needs. For example, a borough may have mosques, Catholic churches and synagogues, as well as shops catering to special food preferences and customs of the people within the district.

- Intercultural is something existing or happening between different cultures. In the mentioned case, the existence of different ethnic groups sharing the same space does not guarantee any cultural exchange between them. The city of Toledo in the 15th century was an example of a inter-cultural society in which Muslims, Catholics and Jews not only lived together harmoniously but also studied and created together.

Knowing these two, Mietusch (2015) suggests a third term: *transculturality*, which refers to "the act of linking cultures and overcoming cultural gaps in the process". By contrast, the concepts of intercultural and multicultural both emphasise the differences between cultures.

In a reality where the world has become globalised, where knowledge flows through the web, where the possibility of virtual training sessions has increased, taking note of the phenomenon of *hyperconnectivity*, and of the relevance of considering it *transcultural*, is essential.

A few years ago it became possible to have clients in different parts of the world, as well as to be part of a team of facilitators in global coaching training, to take certifications with colleagues on the American continent and to work with one's supervisor located on another continent. All this within a week or even a single day. Life and education are no longer necessarily located in the place where one is physically present. Virtual experiences have allowed us to be present in many parts of the world in a way that was undreamed of just a couple of decades ago.

Since the beginning of the Covid-19 pandemic, this change has only accelerated and has probably become irreversible. Virtual interaction has acquired the same weight as physical presence in many fields of human experience, at least in terms of management and decision-making. It is therefore necessary to address the transcultural part of its content and to explore the existence of transcultural humour. *Transcultural* humour may need to be content-specific, as humour needs to be based on shared context. In addition to context, it will also be necessary to consider the quality of the relationship.

# Transitional space. A sense of playfulness

Humour requires the light feeling of play. It is not just about fun, it is more related to what Winnicott called Transitional Space. The feeling of healthy complicity and private jokes. The kind of connection when one says a word and the other understands and maybe no one else does, but is part of the link between the pair, it is the possibility to have in a shared language, as it was a secret code. But how do we get there? What are the dynamics inside this relationship?

As said before, there is general ambivalence about introducing words like *play* and *humour* in professional life. So it would be normal that we would follow the same trend in coaching and coaching supervision.

One of the first barriers to think about play and humour is the fear of being "silly". Socially, silly can be close to being stupid, only less serious. For example, the silly gifts that show that we think of someone, the silly song we dedicate, the silly love we fall for, the silly gesture showing that we care, silly words that tend to be kind and warm… playing is thus silly. However, at the end, we realise that many of the most important details in life are silly.

Here lies the essence of many important things: in simple things, in absurd things and in nearly naïve things. It is here we find the important gestures of life, as we can see in films such as *Forrest Gump* or *The Gardener* with Peter Sellers. A vision not touched by malice, full of tenderness and which arises emotional response due to its profound spontaneity (Chapter 2). This is how discoveries are made: often ingenious, full of tenderness, accompanied by a smile and when joined by surprise, with a big laugh.

# Why do coaching and supervision in coaching require us to be playful?

To answer this question first we must define what playing is. Definitions are very important in these matters, for if it is not done correctly, it can miss the intended meaning. According to the Cambridge Dictionary, the definition of play is:

As a verb:   * When you play a sport or game, you compete or are involved
            in it
          * When children play they enjoy themselves with toys or games
          * To make music with a musical instrument
          * To be a character in a film or play

As a noun: * A story that is written for actors to perform
          * Things that people, especially children, do to enjoy
          themselves

There is a great gap between all of the above definitions and the actual feeling of playing. The description of playing is far removed from the experience of playing.

Actually, Coaches often use *ice-breakers*, which are little tasks or a series of instructions with questions that allow the participants in a gathering or workshop to enter a different space and disconnect from the context from which they join a meeting.

With this, we are consciously trying to get the participants to pay full attention to the process. It is interesting that this is exactly what playing does, as there is the interaction between mind and body.

Then playing is not about having fun: playing is about living in the present. The play thus has a place in Supervision because in general terms playing is not "inside" or "outside", it is in the creative space of two people playing together. This thinking originates with Winnicott who, in his book *Playing and Reality* (1971), describes psychotherapy in the following way:

> Psychotherapy takes place in the overlap of two areas of playing: that of the patient and that of the therapist. Psychotherapy has to do with two people playing together.

(p. 80)

Winnicott worked with 60,000 children over his lifetime, both as a paediatrician and as a psychoanalyst, so he lived the health and sickness of children very closely, and this allowed him to infer that something that was happening to the children could also be found in adults:

> Whatever I say about children playing really applies to adults as well, the distinction being that issues are more difficult to describe when

the patient's material appears mainly in terms of verbal communication. I suggest that we must expect to find playing just as evident in the analyses of adults as it is in the case of our work with children. It manifests itself, for instance, in the choice of words, in the inflections of the voice, and indeed in the sense of humour.

(p. 65)

*It is play that is universal*, and it belongs to health: playing facilitates growth and therefore health; playing leads to group relationships; playing can be a form of communication in psychotherapy would say Winnicott. And I would add that playing is a way of being together, whether in psychotherapy, the helping profesisions and particularly in coaching supervision.

# Looking at playing through the Seven-Eye Model

Now I would like to connect playing with a very precise point in Supervision. As we mentioned before, Coaching Supervision takes place in a system in which there are various relationships apart from the Supervisor and the Coach. There are the relations with the coach's client, with the surroundings and all the many different levels of interaction within this space. To help untangle this complexity, it is necessary to bring in the "Seven-Eye" supervision model developed by Hawkins (2012), in which he identifies the following interactions of the relationship:

The seven-eye supervisor model

Mode 1: Focus on the client and his present

Mode 2: Exploration of the strategies and interventions used by the supervisee

Mode 3: Focusing on the relationship between the client and the supervisee

- Attending to the client's transference
- Learning from the unconscious supervision of the client

Mode 4: Focus on the supervisee

Mode 5: Focus on the supervisory relationship

Mode 6: The supervisor focusing on his own internal process
Mode 7: Focusing on the wider contexts in which the work happens
(p. 85).

During the supervision session, it is palpable that play is the key to a successful implementation of Mode 5 in the Seven-Eye model. At the beginning of the session, the focus is on the client (eye 1), and then on the eyes 2, 3 and 4 in which the supervisor points out the coach in several aspects: in the way, he (the coach) interacts and relates to the client and also how he feels about all that is going on. Then we reach **eye 5**. This is the moment when the supervisor starts to analyse the relation between him and the coach. That is, he puts into practice the exercise in the present, recognising in his own person what he has asked the supervisee to reflect about his relation to the client. At this point, we can find the phenomenon of the Parallel Process, that is to say, an activation of the unconscious in the client's conduct that can be "reenacted" by the coach in the supervision relationship. For example, if the client is very reserved and reticent, at a certain moment these traits can appear in the coach when he finds himself in the space of supervision, and he might show scepticism in conversation or appear closed in the interventions and questions coming from the supervisor. It is very important in the process of coaching supervision that the supervisor can express this in words so as to be able to use them in the space for reflection. For this, it is essential that the supervisor has carried out important work on himself, so that he can identify his emotions and thoughts and, at a certain moment, can separate from them in order to observe from a different perspective, as if looking at himself from above, far away and outside the system.

Therefore, in the terms we have presented about play in supervision, it is the interaction and interplay of two worlds creating a third space (a transitional space). A space that, even if it is a parallel process, it is also new because not only does it repeat what has happened between client and coach, but helps to achieve a different goal through the subjectivity adopted by the supervisor. **Eye 5** is about the coach, the supervisor and the relationship between them.

**Eye 5** is one of the most difficult to master in coaching supervision. I've witnessed and participated in the experience of forming supervisors, and I have observed that the supervisors in training are so worried about the method, the questions to ask and what they themselves are feeling (which would be eye 6) that they are not able to create a third space; they cannot manage to enter this space in which a relation between both (the coach and the supervisor) can be generated. Therefore, they are clearer about their own emotions than about the details and character of the relation that is being generated in front of them. Practitioners tend to focus more on eye 6, which consists in being aware of the internal emotional and mental processes that they are experiencing, and this helps them during the interaction with the supervisee to recognise the moments of stress they are having because of their self-demanding attitude about performing well. Nevertheless, focusing so much on this process is preventing them from generating a relation that requires a certain presence that allows the unfolding of a relation that could be analysed by **eye 5**. That is, the focus on self could be generating a self-absorption that disallows a real presence and genuine "being with" the other. Playing can be a way to be present to avoid this.

Supervision is a sophisticated way of playing, of being with the other in a space for live reflection. One cannot play if not present. When a child and an adult play together, if one is not present the other has to do the "task" for the two, and the experience of playing is not satisfactory. When one actor is inhibited to play, whether in a children's game or in a supervision relationship, what is missing is the *presence*. Supervision requires being able to be present for oneself and for the other at the same time. Hawkins (Turner and Palmer, 2019) has also pointed out the following, as to the presence of the supervisor:

> Mindfulness can be used in supervision to invite the supervisee to focus less on theoretical rehearsed narratives of what happened in their coaching work and instead on what is happening to them in the present as they recall their work.
>
> (p. 73)

There is also another way of presenting oneself in supervision and it is through the possibility of the supervisor thinking of the learning process, in the experience he will have in the encounter of supervision. Hawkins continues that (Turner and Palmer, 2019) the supervisor knows that he is going into the session to play:

As supervisors, it is helpful to tap into this renewable energy within us and in the wider field. We need to enter the supervision space with an open mind, open heart and open will, curious about what stories will emerge as well as what new insights and ways of responding.

(pp. 92–93)

As Mietusch suggests, to successfully understand and enjoy humour across cultures, the humour creator must not only be aware of social conventions but also adapt to communication as well as select content, sense the opportunity and carefully create a good punchline.

However, we need to identify what type of humour is being produced, so that we can translate it for the supervisee and also pass it through analysis of eye 7 model as in the mechanism, is activated in the relation of the two participants – supervisor and supervisee. Nor is humour possible when there is tension or intense formality between the participants in the relation. In fact, the lack of the presence of humour in some of the sessions indicates a certain rigidity in the supervision relation, which ought to lead to the supervision of the coach supervisor himself.

# Presence and active listening

There is a clear difference between being present and showing up. In the field of coaching and coaching supervision, being present refers to using the whole self as an instrument for understanding and connecting with the other. This "actual presence" is becoming increasingly important in our fast-paced world, where presence is being "stolen" by mobiles, monitors and neverending work agendas. Eunice Aquilina (Turner and Palmer, 2019) proposes using the self as an instrument, based on certain teachings from Antiquity. This includes a series of stages for connecting with the client. Among them: is *Going inside,* as a first step to getting in touch with oneself, being sensitive to our own moods and emotions. From there, we go to *Understanding* what is the client's narrative, holding a space for him and letting compassion be present. Also, relative to our topic, *Embody empathy* for trust and resilience to build and develop. It is this rich world of emotions, narrative (both expressed and unspoken) and trust that constitutes the necessary context for humour.

**Coaching presence** is one of the key competencies for International Coaching Federation (ICF) and it is described as *the ability to be fully conscious and create a spontaneous relationship with the client, employing a style that is open, flexible and confident.* Interestingly, for a proficient coach, this includes *the ability to use humour effectively to create lightness and energy.*

**Active listening** is part of the ICF Effective Communication Competencies and it is best described as the ability to completely focus on what the client is both saying and not saying. The goal is twofold: to understand the meaning of what is being said by the client in the context of his desires, and to support his self-expression.

In a humorous way, a dear friend shared this in his blog:

- *Hey, I want to ask you for advice.*
- *Tell me.*
- *Things have been very tense with my girlfriend.*
- *So cut off the relationship.*
- *But we have been together for a long time.*
- *Well, stay with her.*
- *But I really despair with these things going on.*
- *Then cut it off.*
- *But we know each other so well.*
- *Well, stay with her.*
- *But lately she's been so nagging.*
- *Then cut it off.*
- *But then I remember she has always supported and adviced me.*
- *Well, stay with her.*
- *It just dawned on me, why she could be like this recently.*
- *Well?*
- *Because she's afraid of this new business I want to try.*
- *And?*
- *Well, she has experience in that, but I didn't ask for her advice.*
- *Ah, see!*
- *I'll talk to her.*
- *You would do well.*
- *Ah, thank you very much! You give the best advice in the world!*
- *Eh… you're welcome.*

Some people rarely have the experience of truly being listened to. Generally, to be able to listen to someone, one must have been listened to by someone else. Most of the time it is the parents or primary caretakers who become the first listeners, sometimes teachers in the early years of education. Being listened to is as important as being seen: it is a way of feeling loved and appreciated. In coaching and supervision, listening is the beginning of the connection: it builds the way that interactions are felt, and the space coaches leave for the silence. There is also listening to the tone and the quality of the words that are chosen. Sometimes listening also means interrupting in order to clarify or question an unseen option worth exploring. Active listening, like presence, is only possible through our full, undivided attention. Hence, the possibility of introducing the right story hangs on listening intently to both the words that are spoken and the ones that remain unsaid. Humour can help bring hidden meaning to the surface.

# How to introduce humour into the session?

We should consider that one of the elements of playing is humour and that it starts with the use of words, images and metaphors.

Freud considers that humour is a highly refined mechanism of defence of the human psyche, this is why it is important to identify when humour appears in sessions of coaching supervision. I use the word "appear" because humour cannot be forced, nor can one generate instructions to "create" humour. There is nothing less funny than someone who is forcing himself to be funny. However, there are resources that can be useful to the coach and/or supervisor to lighten the conversation.

# Strategies for the use of humour

An important part of the initial conversation about contracting supervision is the recognition of the role sentiments and emotions play in the process. "[We must] recognize that thoughts and emotions are inextricably linked, and that overlooking the impact of emotions would be irresponsible: even neglecting to recognize emotions could prevent critical thought and reflection" (Turner and Palmer, 2019, p. 53).

At this point, we can explore how humour can be generated at any moment – for example, with a pun – as a way of going beyond the stated meaning of the words in the conversation and also as a way of integrating emotions in the context of the process.

Mietusch mentions several strategies in coaching training that can be used in coaching supervision. As a precaution, if the mood or the style of the audience is not known from the beginning, coaches and facilitators should not use humour at the outset of the session, nor in coaching.

We agree in suggesting not using humour in the first session of supervision. However, as the relationship evolves, the supervisor should be attentive to the moods of his client and be ready to use his intuition in order to decide whether it is appropriate or not to use humour. There are stories and anecdotes that can be used to steer the conversation into a lighter mood and propose a change of perspective which can be the start of a relationship. In this respect, strategies are more akin to a recount of experiences than to a procedure manual.

Following Mietusch (2015), who uses it for coaching training – whether individual or in groups – we can see that the supervisor will read the style of the group or person (meaning his humour or disposition) to approach and then adapt to that style, words or expressions. In this sense, the psychological function is to gain a common ground in which the supervisee feels comfortable and listened to at a higher level. Another possibility is that, after the group reading, humour could be introduced in the style of the coach or facilitator. The advantage of the latter is that a new space is created for the supervisee: one that corresponds to what we call the *play area* (Winnicott), but is taken to a social space (Figure 6.2).

## In Tales for Trainers

In *Tales for Trainers*, Parkin (2010) reminds us that telling stories is the most effective way of transmitting a piece of knowledge. It sets a basis that can be used as an example or it can open a new space to think things over. Stories are used for children but they can also be used for the development of leadership among business executives. It works in two ways; first, because it allows them to think about things related to their chores but they are not directed at them as being responsible. The

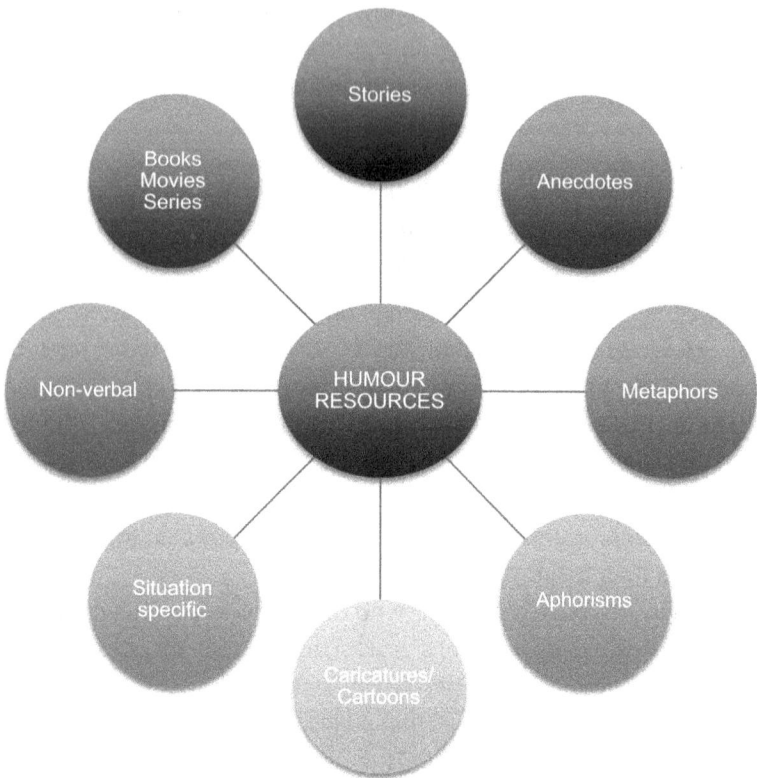

*Figure 6.2* Web diagram that starts from humour resources at the centre surrounded by eight different vehicles to introduce humour in the session.

second is because, accustomed as they are too tedious or repetitive activities, stories send them back to those childhood moments when they liked to listen to their parents or grandparents and therefore they relax. Who doesn't like to listen to a story?

According to Parkin (2010, p. 12), a story is the account of an incident that can be real or imaginary. "Although the hero or heroine might be as far-ranging as a chief executive of a company, an all-powerful goddess, or a set of streetwise pigs, the format of stories is basically the same: characters, plot, conflict and resolution".

When thinking about supervision, group or individual, we can see that when the persons enjoy sharing a humorous story and laugh together, tension dispels and a different individual attitude develops within the system or group.

In supervision, as soon as the listener can identify with the hero or heroine or with the problems that they are dealing with, they can enter into a more creative space.

Example

What the Sleeping beauty would have given her right arm for?

This princess was different. She was a brunette beauty with a genius of a brain. Refusing marriage, she inherited all by primo-genesis. The country's economy prospered under her rule. When the handsome prince came by on his white charger, she bought it from him and started her own racehorse business. Zoe Ellis (Parkin, 2010, p. 88).

Another clear example would be Mulla Nasrudin's stories, as narrated by Idries Shah (2015). These tales are full of surprises and paradoxes that defy common understanding. Therefore a gap for new connotations opens and further knowledge can come in.

*Why don't you?*
*Nasrudin went to the shop of a man who stocked all kinds of bits and pieces.*
*Have you got nails?" he asked.*
*"Yes".*
*"And leather, good leather?"*
*"Yes".*
*"And twine?"*
*"Yes".*
*"And dye?"*
*"Yes".*
*"Then why, for Heaven's sake, don't you make a pair of boots?"*


*The Use of a Light*
*"I can see in the dark", boasted Nasrudin one day in the teahouse.*
*"If that is so, why do we sometimes see you carrying a light through the streets?"*
*"Only to prevent other people from colliding with me".*


Peter Hawkins (2005) in *The Wise Fool's Guide to Leadership* takes the character of Nasrudin and makes him a leadership consultant. What can be particularly useful in the Supervision of Coaching are stories dedicated to "unlearning", which is defined as the "process by which organizations unlock the evolving of their culture" (p. 51). Unlearning is not about finding the correct answer, but rather about discovering objective, subjective or inter-subjective possibilities that may not have been there before the session of supervision. Also, the value of mistakes as the best vehicle for learning, like in the following story about Nasrudin.

*Example*

*Right the first time*

*Nasrudin was invited to attend a major company programme to improve quality. As he walked down the corridor to visit one of the programme workshops he could hear people chanting RIGHT FIRST TIME – EVERY TIME – WITH ZERO DEFECTS*

*Nasrudin turned to his host and said,*

> *How sad that this group have been deprived of the food of failure, but I am sure that God will notice their deprivation and send them some.*
>
> (p. 59)

*Success*

*Nasrudin was at a conference with other management consultants. The others were all staying at the most expensive hotel and going out each evening to the best restaurants in town. Nasrudin was sitting in the conference hall eating his plain bread and cheese. One of his colleagues came up to him and said:*

> "If only you would learn to tell the companies what they want to hear and were less confrontational, then you would earn better fees and would not have to be left here eating plain bread and cheese". Nasrudin replied: "if you would learn to live on bread and cheese then you would not have to spend your time telling companies what you think they want to hear".
>
> (p. 58)

*How did you become so clever?*

*One day Nasrudin was asked:*

*"How did you learn to become so clever?"*

*"It was quite easy", he replied. "I just talked a lot and when I saw people nodding their head in agreement, I wrote down what I had said".*

## Metaphors

A metaphor is described as a word or phrase used to describe something, in a way that is different from its normal use, in order to show that the two things have the same qualities and to make the description more powerful.

Metaphors can be used in two different ways: as a means of communication or as ways of exploration, although sometimes they are interrelated.

1. Metaphors as ways of communicating a thought

In a learning context, metaphors can be a powerful and innovative way of describing a situation, experience or problem that can offer alternative information, help the listener to re-frame or see that situation in a different light, and hopefully provide them with additional ways of resolving it (Parkin, 2010, p. 17). They also can have a more dramatic effect on the listener than literal language.

Listening to a metaphor serves to interrupt a pattern. It can be startling, so as to force us to shift from our habitual thinking and help us comprehend what is not immediately evident.

2. Metaphors as exploration

We can think of this as the technique of Clean Language created by David Grove, who invites us to use the natural expressions of the client or supervisee to tell about his experience. Such as "I'm going round in circles" or "I'm tied up in knots". Usually in social relations, the recipient takes the phrase in its general sense and the conversation continues. In supervision and coaching – which is where the methodology of Clean Language arises– instead of leaving it in its figurative sense we look for the literal sense of these expressions. For example, I've been going round in circles for years, the question is What kind of circles? (Way, 2013, pp. 68–69). The inner world of the client (supervisee) will react and it will lead to an immediate insight. Often metaphors are used to bring to the surface positions or images that the supervisee did not know he had in him. Similarly, it helps to express in a metaphor what could not be expressed in any other way. In this context, beyond the methodology of Clean Language some questions might be:

- If you were an animal, what animal would you be?
- If you were a country, which country would you be?

And among these other metaphors could be used to cause surprise and a certain movement towards humour.

- If you were a piece of furniture in your home and your client another, what would you be?
- If you were a toy and your client another, what toys would you be?
- If you were a finger and your client another, what fingers would you be?

Another example of the use of metaphors in Supervision of Coaching is the Magic Box, which can become part of the technique depending on the mood of the session. The Magic Box as described by Lily Seto and Tina Geithner is a tiny metal box

> that contains small objects with which clients build and explore their metaphoric landscape in relation to a question, topic or scenario. The coach or coaching supervisor facilitates a discovery-based process using direct, succinct, open-ended questions to support clients in unpacking and examining the content and context of their landscape.
>
> (Seto, Geithner, 2018)

## Aphorisms

As used by Peter Hawkins shares in his *13 NEW Crackers for Systemic Team Coaches Christmas 2020*. He shares these aphorisms every year for the purpose of amusing but also because of the learning process.

Don't ask. Don't tell

Coaches can become addicted to questions and consultants to telling the answers. The team coach needs to avoid both addictions and instead engage in collaborative inquiry, facing the challenges that life is presenting, where neither coach nor coachees have the answer, but together are discovering one.

Never know better; Never know first

The best insights are co-discovered fresh between the team and the team coach. Pre-packaged knowledge is hard to both digest and own (Hawkins, 2020).

## Caricatures/Cartoons

There are no specific cartoons for humour in coaching. However, there are various comic strips that can share real-life situations and allow psychological relief and learning. We can think of the likes of *Calvin and Hobbes* by Bill Watterson or *The Far Side* by Gary Larsen. In Latin America, there is *Mafalda* by Quino. All these strips feature characters that question and point out moments in real life, often in deep and poignant ways, that are too easily taken for granted.

## Situation-specific

For situational humour, we can refer back to the pandemic-related jokes by @SoVeryBritish. What can we do differently from everything one can do at home when one was not prepared to be at home?

VeryBritish Problems (@SoVeryBritish)

Trying to come up with an idea for an activity that isn't "eat another biscuit". 29/04/20. 11:47. Tweet

## Non-verbal

During supervision, there is a somatic experience. The body is part of the session, independent of whether its presence is physical or virtual – even in a phone call, it will be present through the tone of the voice and its inflections. Visual contact can convey emotional states: a smile, a grin, a look or a twitch are all indications of "amusement" that relate to what we consider humour in supervision. At this point, transculturalism can be limited, as described by Lily Seto in *Diversity and Inclusion in Supervision*: In Western cultures, an ability to keep eye contact is seen as evidence of confidence and trustworthiness, while in many other cultures, it is considered rude for those of lower status to keep eye contact with those of higher status. That is why it is important to create an initial space of confidence, in which the non-verbal language of both participants can fall into a new, common style. Let us always remember that supervision is a space that allows for creativity.

## Books, movies and series

Movies and particularly series have become a common referent between different regions and generations, just as literature used to be a great store of information – above all of stories and anecdotes – which would be part of the personal baggage of the supervisor. I do not wish to omit an example that relates to both goal-setting and self-awareness, motivation and leadership:

> …*The Cat only grinned when it saw Alice. It looked good-natured, she thought: still it had very long claws and a great many teeth, so she felt that it ought to be treated with respect.*
> *"Cheshire Puss", she began, rather timidly, as she did not at all know whether it would like the name. However, it only grinned a little wider.*
> *"Come, it's pleased so far" thought Alice, and she went on.*
> *"Would you tell me, please, which way I ought to go from here?"*
> *"That depends a good deal on where you want to get to", said the Cat.*
> *"I don't much care where-" said Alice.*
> *"Then it doesn't matter which way you go", said the Cat*
> *"-so long as I get somewhere", Alice added as an explanation.*
> *"Oh, you're sure to do that", said the Cat, "if you only walk long enough". Lewis Carroll, 1865.*
> (Parkin, 2010, p. 118)

# Humour dont's

Sarcasm is the type of humour is to be avoided in coaching supervision. It is important to be able to distinguish it as it can present itself in different forms. It can be very corrosive for the participants, as it indicates an unconscious mechanism of defence (later on we shall see forms of humour suggested that can lead to reflection or internal growth). Among the types of sarcasm that the coaching and coaching supervisor should guard against, because of the harm they inflict, we find the following (Figure 6.3):

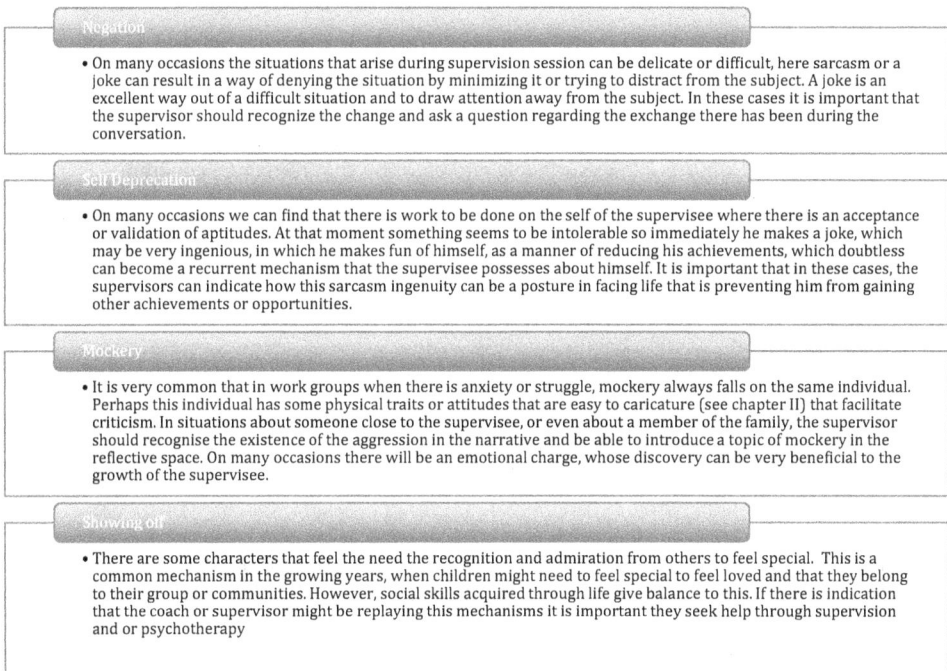

**Negation**

- On many occasions the situations that arise during supervision session can be delicate or difficult, here sarcasm or a joke can result in a way of denying the situation by minimizing it or trying to distract from the subject. A joke is an excellent way out of a difficult situation and to draw attention away from the subject. In these cases it is important that the supervisor should recognize the change and ask a question regarding the exchange there has been during the conversation.

**Self Deprecation**

- On many occasions we can find that there is work to be done on the self of the supervisee where there is an acceptance or validation of aptitudes. At that moment something seems to be intolerable so immediately he makes a joke, which may be very ingenious, in which he makes fun of himself, as a manner of reducing his achievements, which doubtless can become a recurrent mechanism that the supervisee possesses about himself. It is important that in these cases, the supervisors can indicate how this sarcasm ingenuity can be a posture in facing life that is preventing him from gaining other achievements or opportunities.

**Mockery**

- It is very common that in work groups when there is anxiety or struggle, mockery always falls on the same individual. Perhaps this individual has some physical traits or attitudes that are easy to caricature (see chapter II) that facilitate criticism. In situations about someone close to the supervisee, or even about a member of the family, the supervisor should recognise the existence of the aggression in the narrative and be able to introduce a topic of mockery in the reflective space. On many occasions there will be an emotional charge, whose discovery can be very beneficial to the growth of the supervisee.

**Showing off**

- There are some characters that feel the need the recognition and admiration from others to feel special. This is a common mechanism in the growing years, when children might need to feel special to feel loved and that they belong to their group or communities. However, social skills acquired through life give balance to this. If there is indication that the coach or supervisor might be replaying this mechanisms it is important they seek help through supervision and or psychotherapy

*Figure 6.3* Bar chart with four ways in which humour should be prevented.

# Humour assessment model for reflective practice

Reflective practice (Hay, 2007) is the review of the coach or supervisor's practice across the past, present or future. Based on this practice, I suggest this model to reflect, particularly after a session where humour was present. It could be a guide for beginners, or for seasoned practitioners that are curious about introducing humour into their sessions if they have not yet done so yet.

This model includes the characteristics of the client and the relationship, the context, the effects of humour content and the mood at the end of the session (Figure 6.4).

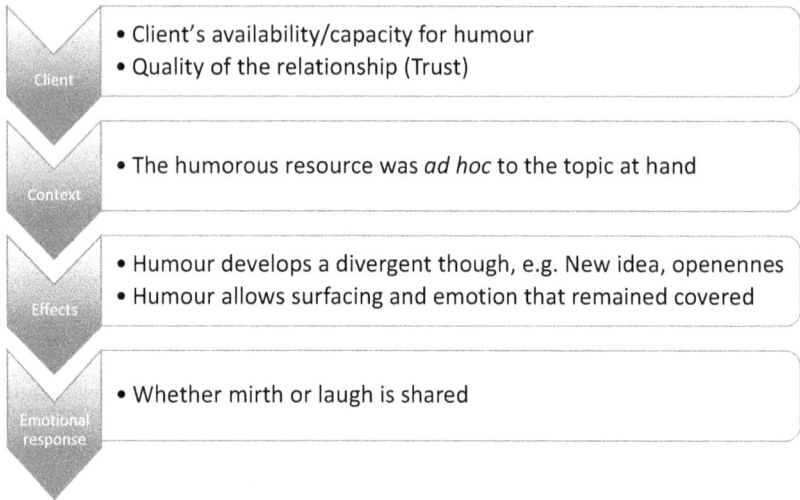

**Client**
- Client's availability/capacity for humour
- Quality of the relationship (Trust)

**Context**
- The humorous resource was *ad hoc* to the topic at hand

**Effects**
- Humour develops a divergent though, e.g. New idea, openennes
- Humour allows surfacing and emotion that remained covered

**Emotional response**
- Whether mirth or laugh is shared

*Figure 6.4* Flux diagram with four steps to reflect on humour.

## Client

Humour brings people together and helps them connect. However, it is important to first know whether the client has the capacity and willingness for humour. Therefore it is suggested to start by aiming humour at oneself and see the reaction of the other: if he joins in, maybe there is space for further humour. The other aspect is the quality of the relationship, when there is a space for the trust it is easier to take the risk.

## Context

It is important to make sure that the content of a joke is relevant to the context. Sometimes the coach or supervisor makes a personal association of ideas, more related to a story of his own, than to the narrative of the client. It is important to reflect on this because this kind of misfire might unnecessarily divert the focus of the conversation, even if the relationship and the mood are good.

## Effect

One of the most important effects of humour is to produce a *divergent thought*. This means that as a result of the humorous intervention, a different train of thought opens up: either as an insight, a new idea, or a new field of exploration. It could also be this particular kind of silence that announces that a new understanding is around the corner. The divergent thought might be evident in the session, but it also can make its appearance later, when the client is by himself.

## Emotional mood

A shared laugh is the perfect closing to the process of using humour. This mirth can also be the expression of a new, shared understanding, of a feeling of something connecting between minds, and of the affection that comes with sharing a new insight.

If you feel comfortable after reflecting on the outcome of these four issues, then congratulations! You are well on your way to using humour in a confident manner. The more you reflect on it, the better you will become.

We have reviewed different ways in which humour can lead to learning, to unlearning, and to reflection. But it might be even better if nothing were learnt as a recipe which is slated in stone. As Freddy Salas says in his book on methodology, *Humourweaning:* humour is a way to enter the process of thinking in order to clear up doubts but, above all, to generate new doubts (Salas).

We can conclude that in coaching and its supervision, humour can be a tool for self-discovery, for the revelation of the client's and coach's psychological conditions, and particularly important: a key vehicle for learning and growing. Humour is shaped by the personality traits of the person who creates it. Therefore, the coaching supervisor needs to be as attentive to his own emotions and thoughts as to those of his client, to constantly assess what is the best intervention and whether humour can fit.

It is essential that each supervisor gathers his own collection of supervision tools. He also needs to know what are the stories, jokes and paradoxes that have moved him the most, because they can be more effectively used to communicate mysteries to reflect upon and, hopefully, solve.

In this way, a new, unknown space will be created for both participants to dwell in, where creativity and respect, play and restraint, will continue to be the most important rules.

# Conclusions

Despite living in a world in which apparently, we have more freedom, we have lost flexibility that was barely in the making. There are modern causes such as the internet and the social networks that seem to have put themselves at the service of ideologies. However, in the field of psychotherapy, there also has always existed an orthodox climate – which various analysts have *rejected* (Kardiner, Winnicott, Balint, Lacan and Meltzer among others). A guardianship environment closer to censorship in which the theoretical questioning was inadmissible. Humour and its appearance in the helping professions sessions have also been met with silence (or indifference?), which makes it difficult to reflect on it and its effects. Humour is part of everyday analytical practice, but it is not very usual to find it mentioned in the scientific writings of the analytical community. The same can be said as regards the field of supervision of coaching. It is a practice that arises precisely in the care of the choice of words required in a very specific moment or time, relevant to the speech of the patient or client.

This is paradoxical because since times of antiquity humour has been an object of interest and intriguing to man. We can say that Aristotle considered that laughter belonged to man, and something uniquely human it should not be left out of the manifestations in links and in sessions. For Baltasar Gracián, wit belongs to the hero, *in the profound meaning of moral philosophy, of lively aesthetics, where man, the original shipwrecked survivor of existence, resorts to reason as a delusive foothold* (Gracián, 1006, p. 9). So that, humour is the way of travelling through life for those heroes! We risk losing humour if we don't allow it to happen, if we do not foster it in our different human practices. We solely need to recognize when it is a sign of growth or when it is used as a barrier for defence.

DOI: 10.4324/9781003154310-8

Humour is a reflection of maturity and development, it is a companion to learning. We do not find it at the beginning of the road, but there are factors at the start of a life that is going to foster laughter and "good nurture". A *sufficiently good mother* can provide support for her child so that it sees the world as interesting and fun. When this support is missing, the baby becomes more focused on its own existential continuity. The loving arms that prolong the contact and warmth of the maternal care, plus the acquisition of speech will allow the child to find pleasure in playing with words. This small human being will discover the gaps in language that lead to confusions and banter, which later will turn into humorous words – a consoling balm for the self.

These are the doors to humour; however, living implies traversing disagreements, frustrations, fantasies, choices and, consequently, losses, so that the presence of sketches of humour in early years does not guarantee in any way its permanence. Of course, there is mature humour that can develop spontaneously – or not, over a lifetime. The special acceptance that people with a good sense of humour have in society shows that to look at life with humour, not a very frequent characteristic, is very much appreciated. Even if developing a sense of humour in the patients is never one of the therapeutic objectives, its development is a manifestation of their passage through analysis. That a patient is able to experience humour, a mature humour, is a sign of the effects of analysis itself. The appearance of humour in supervision of coaching also shows a growth of the self, of confidence, of the ability to laugh at oneself and to use wisdom with the challenges with the clients. The world is getting ever more complex and with more restrictions, being able to play with this without the person feeling overwhelmed by it, is a path towards mental well-being.

Eventhough humour is a spontaneous act, working with humour cannot be unintentional. It is necessary to consider whether humour is of narcissistic benefit to the person of the analyst or the supervisor, as it trails an air of exhibitionism or sadism, which could be detrimental to the subject who has come to talk about himself, his topics, his clients and his fears.

According to several of his patients, Freud himself would intervene in the sessions in various ways and humour was one of them. The anecdotes can vary in quality as they depend on the characteristics of each patient, but among them what is a common truth is that humour transported them, always hit the mark and at the same time consoled them. Freud admired humour and did not hesitate to call it the highest mechanism of defence. But, contrary to repression, it is not a mechanism *par excellence,* since it requires a certain degree of development of the self in order to make use of it.

We can also think of humour during the sessions as a possibility for creating a particular climate where the client, or the coach are able to receive whatever he needs. This is the case of Meltzer, who handles it rather like the music of language and the human voice, the space that is created so that the analyst can work, even as the image of the link between mother and child when it is still in the womb, the music of the mother's voice reaches the baby (Berman de Oelsner and Oelsner, 1999, p. 13). In sessions of supervision, it is used on occasions "The Magic Box" as a way to use forms to play with language, an invitation to find new possible meanings and images that help to think about something that was always there but didn't have words yet.

I like to think about psychoanalysis and supervision, like the most highly refined games for growth of the XXIst century and the sessions where two can meet to form a third place, where what is at stake does not belong to either of them, but rather what is produced there arises from the meeting of the two participants. Humour is a supreme intervention. When it appears in sessions it is neither good nor bad, it is a fleeting product. Humour is elusive and unattainable and can never become a technique, it is unexpected and instantaneous, it is unique and does not require an invitation, it arises apparently out of nothing and it cannot be constructed. It is part of a fundamental change happening in a person arising from profound personal work. One can laugh at oneself only when it is possible to abandon all rigidity of narcissistic trappings.

Humour can be used in teaching and in therapy [...] I link it to maturity to be able to look at the world with interest, passionately and, at the same time, with a little irony about ourselves, as at times we overestimate who we are or what we think (Norberto Bleichmar. Personal Communication).

As Umberto Eco (2000) says

perhaps the task for anyone who loves humanity consists in making them laugh at the truth, making the truth laugh, because the only truth consists in learning to free ourselves from the insane passion for the truth.

(p. 484)

A single truth does not exist. As Peter Hawkins there is never and either or answer, but rather a whole range of possibilities that allow for "the good life" or for us to live well. Within that range is the possibility to humour our life. Humour is like a hand that lifts us up and invites us to go on in spite of the circumstances. Only that the hand is our own self. This is what humour makes possible.

# Bibliography

Baker, R. (1999). *The Delicate Balance between the Use and Abuse of Humor in the Psychoanalytic Setting*, en J. Barron (editor) *Humor and Psych. Psychoanalytic Perspectives*. USA: The Analytic Press.

Baker, R. (1993). *Some Reflections on Humour in Psychoanalysis*. USA: International Journal or Psycho-Analysis.

Bergmann, M.S. (1999). *The Psychoanalysis of Humor and Humor in Psychoanalysis* en J. Barron (editor) *Humor and Psyche. Psychoanalytic Perspectives*. USA: The Analytic Press.

Bergson, H. (1939). *La risa*. Argentina: Losada.

Berman de Oelsner, M., Oelsner, R. (1999). *Entrevista a Donald Meltzer, en Diálogos Clínicos con Donald Meltzer*. Buenos Aires: ApdeBa.

Brabant, E., Falzeder, E., Giampieri-Deutsch, P. (2001). *Sigmund Freud – Sandor Ferenczi Correspondencia completa 1908–1911*, Vol. I.1. Spain: Editorial Síntesis.

Bracht, R., Goulet-Cazé, M.O. *et al.* (2000). *Los cínicos*. Spain: Seix Barral.

Breton, A. (1991). *Antología de Humor Negro*. Spain: Anagrama.

Britton, R. (2003). *Sex, Death, and the Superego. Experiences in Psychoanalysis*. Londres: Karnak.

Burckhard, J. (1999). *La Cultura del Renacimiento en Italia*. Mexico: Sepan Cuantos.

Chesterton, G.K. (2006). *Correr tras el propio sombrero (y otros ensayos)*. Spain: Ed. Acantilado.

Diaz, G., Brück, C. (1988). *Acerca del Humor*. Argentina: Tekne.

Dolto, F. (2001). *A propósito de la función simbólica de las palabras* en *En el Juego del deseo*. Mexico: S. XXI editores.

Doolittle, H. (1956). *Tribute To Freud: With Unpublished Letters By Freud*. USA: Ed. Kessinger Publishing bajo licencia Pantheon Books, Inc., EEUU.

Dupont, H. (1999). *The Delicate Balance between the Use and Abuse of Humor in the Psychoanalytic Setting*, en J. Barron (editor) *Humor and Psyche. Psychoanalytic Perspectives*. USA. The Analytic Press.

Eco, U. (2000). *El Nombre de la Rosa*. Spain: Lumen.

Etchegoyen, R.H. (2002). *Los fundamentos de la Técnica Analítica*. Argentina: Amorrortu.

Ferenczi, S. (2001). *Teoría y Técnica del psicoanálisis*. Argentina: Lumen-Horme.

Ferreter Mora, J. (1994). *Diccionario de Filosofía, Tomo II*. Spain: Ariel.

Flem, L., (2002). *Freud et ses patients*. Paris: Hachette, Paris.

Freud, A. (1993). *Normalidad y Patología en la Niñez*. Mexico: Paidos.

Freud, A. (1961). *El yo y los mecanismos de defensa*. Mexico: Ed. Paidos.

Freud, E., Freud, L., Grubrich-Simitis, I. (2006). *Sigmund Freud. Lieux, visages, objets*. Italy: Éditions Complexe/Éditions Gallimard.

Freud, S. (1980). *Consejos al médico en el tratamiento Psicoanalítico, en Obras Completas*. Spain: Biblioteca Nueva.

Freud, S. (1980). *El Chiste y su relación con el inconsciente, en Obras Completas*. Spain: Biblioteca Nueva.

Freud, S. (1980). *El Hombre de las Ratas, Los casos de S. Freud*. Nueva Visión: Argentina, 2005.

Freud, S., (1980). *El Humor*, Obras Completas, *Tomo III*. Spain: Biblioteca Nueva.

Freud, S. (1980). *El Yo y el Ello*, Obras completas, *Tomo III*. Spain: Biblioteca Nueva.

Freud, S. (1980). *Estudios sobre la histeria, en Obras Completas*. Spain: Biblioteca Nueva.

Freud, S. (1980). *Introducción al Narcisismo, en Obras Completas*. Spain: Biblioteca Nueva.

Freud, S. (1980). *La iniciación del tratamiento, en Obras Completas*. Spain: Biblioteca Nueva.

Freud, S. (1980). *Más allá del principio del placer, Obras Completas*. Spain: Biblioteca Nueva.

Fry, W., Salameh, W. (2004). *El humor y el bienestar en las intervenciones clínicas*. Spain: Desclée de Brower.

Giovacchini, P.L. (1999). *Humor, the Transicional Space and the Therapeutic Process* en J. Barron (editor) *Humor and Psyche. Psychoanalytic Perspectives*. USA. The Analytic Press.

Glover, E. (1930). The 'Vehicle' of Interpretations. *Int. J. Psychoanal.*, 11:340–344.

Goetschy, C. (2008). *El super yo en la teoría psicoanalítica* (Master Thesis Centro Eleia).

Gottlieb, R.M. (1989). Technique and Countertransference in Freud's Analysis of the Rat Man. *Psychoanal. Q.*, 58:29–62.

Gracián, B. (1996). *Agudeza y Arte de Ingenio*. Mexico: Universidad Nacional Autónoma de México.

Greenberg, J. (1998). *Theoretical Models and the Analyst's Neutrality, en Relational Psychoanalysis: The Emergence of a Tradition*. USA: The Analytic Press.

Greenson, R.R. (1972). The Voice of the Intellect Is a Soft One-A Review of The Writings of Anna Freud, Volume IV 1945–1956. *Int/ J. Psychoanal.*, 53:403–417.

Hay, J. (2007). *Reflective Practice and Supervision for Coaches*. Poland: Mc Graw Hill. Open University Press.

Hawkins, P. (2020). 13 NEW Crackers for Systemic Team Coaches Christmas 2020. https://www.renewalassociates.co.uk/2020/12/13-new-crackers-for-systemic-team-coaches-christmas-2020/

Hawkins, P. (2005). *The Wise Fool's Guide to Leadership*. UK: O books.

Hawkins, P., Shohet, R. (2012). *Supervision in the Helping Professions*. UK: McGraw Hill Companies.

Hoffman, I.Z. (1998). *Ritual and Spontaneity in the Psychoanalytic Process*. USA: The Analytic Press.

Jenofonte, (2000). *El Banquete*. Mexico. Porrua. Col. Sepan Cuantos.

Joubert, J.L. (2002). *Tratado de la Risa*. Spain: Asociación Española de Neuropsiquiatría.

Kardiner, A. (1979). *Mi Análisis con Freud*. Mexico: Joaquín Mortiz.

Klein, M. (2003). *Amor, culpa y reparación* en Obras Completas, *Tomo I*. Spain: Paidos.

Klein, M. (2003). *Relato del psicoanálisis de un niño, en Obras Completas, Tomo 4*. Spain: Paidos.

Kohut, H. (1966). Forms and Transformations of Narcissism. *J. Am. Psychoanal. Assn.*, 14:243–272.

Kris, E. (1964). *Psicoanálisis de lo cómico y psicología de los procesos creadores, 2da. Edición*. Argentina: Paidos.

Kubie, L.S. (1971). The Destructive Potential of Humor in Psychotherapy. *Am. J. Psychiatry*, 127:861–866.

Kundera, M. (1994). *Los testamentos traicionados*. Spain: Tusquets.

Lacan, J. (1999). *Seminario Las Formaciones del Inconsciente*. Argentina: Paidos.

Laercio, D. (2006). *Vida de los Filósofos Más Ilustres*. México: Grupo Editorial Tomo.

Laplanche, J., Pontalis, J.B. (1993). *Diccionario de Psicoanálisis*. Argentina: Paidos.

Mahler, M., Pine, F., Bergmann, A. (2002). *El nacimiento psicológico del infante humano*. Mexico: Enlace Editorial.

Meltzer, D. (1978). Routine and Inspired Interpretations—Their Relation to the Weaning Process in Analysis. *Contemp. Psychoanal.*, 14:210–225.

Minois, G. (2000). *Histoire du rire et de la dérision*. Francia: Fayard.

Molière, J.B.P. (2005). *Les femmes savantes*. Spain: Folio classique.

Moliner, M. (1998). *Diccionario de uso del español*. Spain: Gredos.

Ortiz., E. (2011), La mente en desarrollo Reflexiones sobre clinica pscioanalitica. Editorail Paidós.

Parkin, M. (2010). *"Tales for Trainers. Using Stories and Metaphors to Facilitate Learning*. India: Kogan Page.

Poland, W.S. (1990). The Gift of Laughter: On the Development of a Sense of Humor in Clinical Analysis. *Psychoanal. Q.*, 59:197–225.

Pollock, J. (2003). *¿Qué es el humor?* Argentina: Paidós Diagonales.

Rabelais, (2005). *Gargantúa y Pantagruel*. Colombia: Panaméricana.

Reik, T. (1994). *Psicoanálisis del humor judío*. Argentina: Leviatán.

Riebel, L. (1984). Paradoxical Intention Strategies: A Review of Rationales. *Psychother. Theory Res. Pract.*, 21(2):260–272.

Roudinesco, E., Plon, M. (1998). *Diccionario de Psicoanálisis*. Argentina: Paidos.

Rouvière, J. (2005). *Dix siècles d'humour dans la litterature Française*. Francia: Plon.

Salas, F. (2018). Hu*morweaning. Coaching con humor. El humor al servicio del desarrollo de competencias*. Kindle Book.

Sanville, J.B. (1999). *Humor and Play en Humor and Psyche*. USA: The Analytic Press.

Seto, L., Geithner, T. (2018). *Metaphor Magic in Coaching and Coaching Supervision*. https://americassupervisionnetwork.com/journal-article-on-magic-box/

Shah, I. (2015). *The Pleasantries of the Incredible Mulla Nasrudin*. UK: ISF Publishing.

Stern, L. (2007). *Vida y opiniones del Caballero Tristram Shandy*. Spain: Cátedra.

Strachey, J. (1934). The Nature of the Therapeutic Action of Psycho-Analysis. *Int. J. Psycho-Anal.*, 15:127–159.

Way, M. (2013). *Clean approaches for Coaches. How to Create the Conditions for Change using Clean Language & Symbol Modeling*. UK: Clean Publishing.

Winnicott, D.W. (2002). *El Juego* en *Realidad y Juego*. Argentina: Gedisa.

Winnicott, D.W. (2002). *La ubicación de la experiencia cultural* en *Realidad y Juego*. Argentina: Ed. Gedisa.

Winnicott, D.W. (1999). *Objetos y fenómenos transicionales*, en *Escritos de Pediatría y Psicoanálisis*. Spain: Paidos.

Zackehim, V. (2012). *Exit Laughing, How Humour Takes the Sting Out of Death*. USA: North Atlantic Books.

Zwerling, I. (1955). The Favorite Joke in Diagnostic and Therapeutic Interviewing. *Psychoanal. Q.*, 24:104–114.

# Index

Note: *Italic* page numbers refer to figures and page numbers followed by "n" denote endnotes.

For Product Safety Concerns and Information please contact our EU
representative GPSR@taylorandfrancis.com
Taylor & Francis Verlag GmbH, Kaufingerstraße 24, 80331 München, Germany

www.ingramcontent.com/pod-product-compliance
Lightning Source LLC
Chambersburg PA
CBHW050614280326
41932CB00016B/3042

9 780367 723095